RHO DES

T0063747

Travel with Marco Polo
Insider Tips

INSIDER TIP
Your shortcut
to a great
experience

MARCO POLO
TOP HIGHLIGHTS

OLD TOWN ⭐1
Sensible shoes are recommended for strolling through the beautiful lanes.
📷 *Tip: A photograph of the Old Town from the clock tower is almost as good as an aerial shot.*

➤ p. 42, Rhodes Town

MUSEUM OF ARCHAEOLOGY ⭐2
Aphrodite, a fabulous garden and a hospital from the age of the knights – all in one location.
📷 *Tip: The many lion sculptures on the garden's terrace provide good photo opportunities.*

➤ p. 42, Rhodes Town

PALACE OF THE GRAND MASTER ⭐
A palace for the Grand Master of the Knights of Rhodes, now home to the latest archaeological finds.

➤ p. 44, Rhodes Town

MANDRÁKI HARBOUR ⭐
Sailing boats and excursion vessels in one of the most beautiful harbours on the Aegean Sea. Could this have been the location of the Colossus? (photo)
📷 *Tip: Take a photograph of the town from the entrance to the harbour when the lights come on in the evening.*

➤ p. 46, Rhodes Town

NÉA AGORÁ ⭐5

A market building straight from *The Arabian Nights* serves as a refuge from rain, storms or intense sun.

➤ p. 47, Rhodes Town

FILÉRIMOS ⭐6

Some come here to get married, others to watch the landing aeroplanes – but all can enjoy the herb-flavoured liqueur.

➤ p. 55, Rhodes Town

KALLITHÉA SPRINGS ⭐7

A tiny coastal inlet, surrounded by palm trees, and a lovingly restored spa complex.

📷 *Tip: Take your camera into the water to get the best shots.*

➤ p. 56, Rhodes Town

ACROPOLIS OF LÍNDOS ⭐8

A donkey carries you through this picturesque village to the tip of the rocky outcrop with its temple and castle.

📷 *Tip: When you take pictures of people riding, move very close to the donkey's head.*

➤ p. 62, Líndos & the South

ST MARY'S CHURCH ⭐9

A saint with a dog's head? Admire this curiosity and many more among the religious murals of this village church.

➤ p. 64, Líndos & the South

PETALOÚDES ⭐10

In high summer, thousands of butterflies can be found in this magnificent green valley, and even in the local taverna.

➤ p. 88, The Centre

CONTENTS

CONTENTS

⊙	Plan your visit	🍴	Eating/drinking	🌂	Rainy day activities
€ – €€€	Price categories	🛍	Shopping	🐗	Budget activities
(*)	Premium-rate phone number	🍸	Going out	👥	Family activities
		🏖	Top beaches	▐	Classic experiences

A2) Refers to the pull-out map
a2) Refers to the additional map on the pull-out map
0) Located off the map

BEST OF
RHODES

Turquoise sea, pink oleander and white houses all compete for your attention in the bay of Líndos

ACTIVITIES TO BRIGHTEN YOUR DAY

A KNIGHT'S CASTLE STEEPED IN HISTORY

The *Palace of the Grand Master* (photo) in Rhodes Town is an ideal place to while away the time on rainy days, and there is even a cáfe.
➤ p. 44, Rhodes Town

HEAVENLY HOUR

The interior of the *Evangelismós Church* at Mandráki Harbour in the island's capital is completely covered in frescos in the traditional Byzantine style – a perfect opportunity to test your knowledge of the Bible.
➤ p. 46, Rhodes Town

SHELTERED REFUGE

A pleasant place to sit, sheltered from possible wind and rain, is the inner courtyard of the fine market hall *Néa Agorá* in Rhodes Town.
➤ p. 47, Rhodes Town

PERMANENTLY WET

Underwater creatures can be seen close up at the art deco *aquarium* on the northernmost tip of the island, as can other curious animals, such as a one-eyed ape and a calf with seven hoofs.
➤ p. 49, Rhodes Town

HEAD FOR SHELTER

A tourist cannot leave Rhodes without buying an umbrella first – no other island in the Aegean has a larger selection of umbrellas. When it starts to rain, head for the stores around the *Platía Kyprou* in the New Town.
➤ p. 53, Rhodes Town

A GLASS OF WINE

At the winery of the *Triantáfyllou* family, winemaker Jáson invites you to talk shop at an extensive wine tasting. When it stops raining, he will take you on a tour of the vines – on the back of a horse, if you request it.
➤ p. 89, The Centre

BEST ON A BUDGET

FOR SMALLER WALLETS

TOUR OF THE MOAT
A stroll through the park-like *moat* that surrounds Rhodes Old Town will give you an idea of the colossal task facing the Ottoman invaders who laid siege to Rhodes in the 16th century. In contrast to the city walls, access is free and possible at all times (photo).
➤ p. 42, Rhodes Town

PICTURE BOOK OF FAITH
The church in *Thári* Monastery near Láerma is decorated entirely with biblical frescos, which you can enjoy without paying for the privilege. With a bit of luck, you might even be invited to join the monks for a mocha and a sweet snack.
➤ p. 69, Líndos & the South

GREAT PERSPECTIVES – IN EVERY RESPECT
From the *Tsambíka* Monastery, high up above the east coast, you can enjoy one of the finest Rhodes panoramas. Taking a look at the guest book of the monastery's miracle-working Virgin Mary will give you a perspective on the motives of those locals who have made the pilgrimage here.
➤ p. 91, The Centre

CYCLING THROUGH THE FORESTS
From the *Élafos Hotel* on the mountain Profítis Ilias you can borrow a mountain bike for free – even if you're not a guest – and head off into the thick forests that cloak the island's second-highest mountain.
➤ p. 93, The Centre

CONQUERING CASTLES
The strenuous walks to the medieval castles of *Archángelos* and Charáki on the east coast and *Kritinía* and Monólithos on the west are definitely worth it – entrance is free after all.
➤ p. 94 and p. 99, The Centre

BEST WITH CHILDREN

FUN FOR YOUNG & OLD

PORTRAIT ARTISTS

Numerous painters occupy the pavements on the route from Mandráki Harbour (see p. 46) to the Old Town. They will draw people's portraits, either true to life or as a cartoon, depending on the sitter's wishes – a fun alternative to a conventional holiday snap of your child. Prices are negotiable.

MONTE SMITH

In contrast to other ancient sites in Greece, there are no guards waiting to call kids to order if they fancy chasing each other round the track of the reconstructed *stadium* on Monte Smith. High above the town, they can emulate the athletes of antiquity in a truly historic setting. As the site is accessible at all times, you can also choose to come in the cool of early morning or late afternoon.
➤ p.49, Rhodes Town

A WALK IN THE PARK

Rodíni Park has a stream with waterfalls and ponds amid pine, plane and cypress trees. Fallow deer and wild goats are kept in an enclosure, while peacocks strut along the paths. The playgrounds are somewhat run down.
➤ p.49, Rhodes Town

MINIATURE TRAIN

Rhodes has a number of miniature trains called *trenáki*, which run on rubber wheels. Passengers big and small sit in two or three open carriages, and the trains operate on fixed routes.
➤ p70, Líndos & the South and p. 88, The Centre

FÁRMA OF RHODES

The island's only animal park is located in unspoilt countryside near the butterfly valley. Children can pet many of the different species and try omelettes made from ostrich eggs.
➤ p.90, The Centre

A VISIT TO THE SYNAGOGUE

Rounding off the multicultural mosaic that is Rhodes is the *synagogue* in Rhodes Town. Members of the Jewish community, which was re-formed after the Holocaust, give visitors an insight into their history and faith.
➤ p. 46, Rhodes Town

A CLASSIC COFFEEHOUSE

At *Aktaion*, judges and lawyers get together in the mornings while the cream of Rhodian society gather here in the afternoons. There's also a constant stream of people with time on their hands, both young and old.
➤ p. 49, Rhodes Town

FEASTING AT MAMA SOFIA'S

Things that Rhodians love to eat are on the menu in this taverna in Rhodes Town: scary-looking *foúskes* (barnacles) or *simiaká* – tiny shrimps, smaller than the ones you know from home.
➤ p. 50, Rhodes Town

DANCING UNDER THE STARS

Rhodians prefer to spend balmy summer evenings outdoors, and open-air discos are popular. One of the largest is the *Ampitheatre Club* near Líndos, where guests dance under the stars with a magnificent view of the bay and the castle bathed in moonlight.
➤ p. 68, Líndos & the South

PICNIC WITH A VIEW

At the chapel *Ágios Geórgios Kálamos* high above the Aegean Sea, you can enjoy a picnic at tables in the shade of trees with a view across the sea to the neighbouring islands.
➤ p. 75, Líndos & the South

RUSTIC VILLAGE

The mountain village of *Mesanagrós* paints a fine picture of the decline of the island villages in the pre-tourism days of the 20th century (photo).
➤ p. 77, Líndos & the South

GET TO KNOW RHODES

Hanging out at Plimmíri beach

DISCOVER RHODES

Gigantic walls: the Palace of the Grand Master dominates the Old Town

Your descent by plane starts when you reach the Aegean. From the windows the left, the Turkish coastline and Greek islands appear to blend into another. Rhodes then appears out of the sea: the island is not a flat atoll, abounds in forests, mountains and beaches. You are about to land in parad in fact, Parádisi is the name of the village where the airport is located.

INTO TOWN!

If you want to plunge straight into Greek life, your first port of call should be island's capital. The best and cheapest way to travel there is by bus. Depending your bus driver's age and taste, your journey will be accompanied by sounds of Gr rock or traditional folk music. The windscreen is sure to be decorated with family p tos as well as an icon of a saint to protect passengers on their journey.

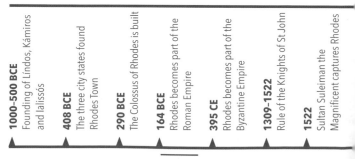

1000–500 BCE
Founding of Líndos, Kámiros and Ialissós

408 BCE
The three city states found Rhodes Town

290 BCE
The Colossus of Rhodes is built

164 BCE
Rhodes becomes part of the Roman Empire

395 CE
Rhodes becomes part of the Byzantine Empire

1309–1522
Rule of the Knights of St John

1522
Sultan Suleiman the Magnificent captures Rhodes

OLD OR NEW TOWN?

On arrival at the capital you have the choice between the ancient and modern, between the city and the sea: on one side are the ramparts and towering fortifications of the Old Town, on the other, shops and boutiques selling the latest fashion labels and umbrellas. There are cafés everywhere, most of which attract a fashionable crowd. Before a shopping trip, take a seat, slow down, soak in the sights and sounds around you. Even if you order another drink, the waiter will often bring a bottle of water for you to quench your immediate thirst. Water is a sign of hospitality and respect to the guest; and "respect" is one of the most important words in the Greek language.

BACK TO THE PAST

Now get ready to take a trip 2,400 years back in time. Leave your high heels back at the hotel though: most of the streets in the Old Town are covered in cobblestones, polished round and smooth over time by hundreds of thousands of feet. No other city, inhabited mainly by Christians, has more mosques and minarets in one small space, and the same applies to medieval houses. The city is also home to Byzantine chapels, an Ottoman hammam, a synagogue, a medieval hospital and the remains of ancient walls. Dotted with a plethora of cafés and tavernas, guesthouses and boutique hotels in ancient buildings, music clubs and shops, yet the city also offers quiet corners for reflection and tiny, narrow streets full of roaming cats.

INSIDER TIP
Avoid high heels

1821-28
The Greek struggle for independence leads to the founding of the new Greek state

1912
The Italians occupy the island

1943
German occupation; the Jewish population is deported

1947
The Dodecanese become Greek

1967-74
Military dictatorship in Greece

1981
Greece becomes a full member of the EU

2008-2018
Greek debt crisis

FINALLY, BEACH VIBES

The sea is the city's other highlight awaiting you. Take a stroll past the yachts, fishing vessels and excursion boats to the beach clubs, where your drink will be served to you as you relax on the sun loungers. You can also laze on the beach or swim over to the diving platform. Here, the views stretch out to the Turkish coastline, which is also worth a day's exploration. Maybe you prefer to catch an hour's rest in preparation for the evening's entertainment: the city comes alive just before midnight, either in the New Town among tourists or in the Old Town among locals in front of two mosques.

OUT & ABOUT ON THE ISLAND

But this is only the start of your journey around Rhodes. The island's history will reveal itself when you head out of the capital to explore the countryside around. Ancient temples and an ancient city, knights' castles, churches and monasteries await you – cultural sites embedded in a stunning landscape. The list of sights and attractions seems endless. You can drive through dense forests where giants appear to have played with large slabs of rock. Or why not visit a taverna in Petaloúdes where the chef is sometimes hidden from view by a swarm of butterflies? There is no such thing as boredom on Rhodes.

A BEACH FOR EVERY TASTE

Rhodes abounds in beaches, and they are just as diverse as the island itself. Faliráki has a wide, fine sandy beach which stretches along the coast for kilometres. Snorkelers prefer the rocky cove which once belonged to the Hollywood star Anthony Quinn. Standing on the main beach of Líndos, there are fantastic views on all sides of the wide bay with the town's ancient acropolis towering above a cascade of whitewashed houses. The Mojito Beach Bar at Gennádi Beach attracts crowds of all-night party-goers who chill out in the day in the hammocks and beach huts. A holiday should always be an expression of freedom, and freedom is highly prized on this island.

ECONOMIC FREEDOM

Rhodes was only granted its freedom, or independence, in 1947. Up until then, it spent many years governed by foreign rulers, a state which many islanders believe they experienced again during the Greek debt crisis: they cannot understand why the austerity measures, imposed on Greece by Europe and the rest of the world, mainly affected the little people. That said, most Rhodians are better off than their neighbours in the big cities on the mainland. You do not see poverty on the streets; the only indication of the island's hard times are the food donation boxes in the supermarkets. Rhodes has kept itself above water mainly thanks to tourism. Locals demonstrate their appreciation and gratitude by showing you their hospitality and kindness.

AT A GLANCE

115,490
population

Isle of Wight: 142,000

4km
of city walls

18km

distance between Rhodes and the Turkish coast

1,400km²
area

Isle of Skye: 1,656km²

HIGHEST PEAK: ATÁVIROS

1,216M

WARMEST MONTH

AUGUST
30.7 °C

RECORD TEMPERATURES

-4°C
Lowest temperature ever recorded in Rhodes Town

DODECANESE

group of islands to which Rhodes belongs

2,776km

linear distance between London and Rhodes

For a while, Anthony Quinn, famous star of *Zorba the Greek*, owned a home and his own private bay on Rhodes

UNDERSTAND RHODES

ANIMAL WELFARE

Oh, how cute they are! And how friendly! Stray dogs and homeless cats are not a rare sight on Rhodes. The animals are harmless, but they have a hard life and go hungry, particularly in winter. The financial crisis also led to a number of pedigree dogs being abandoned in the wild or on refuse tips. Animal welfare societies on the island organise animal transports and adoptions overseas.

BANKS & THE BUILDING BOOM

Before the country was declared bankrupt in 2010, many Greeks were living in a land of milk and honey. Their banks would call regularly encouraging them to take out credit. "What, only 20,000 euros? No, take 50,000 euros instead," the banks would say, knowing full well who owned what land and how much money their clients earned. New building developments were then proposed, making people believe they had sufficient financial means to invest. Many people unfortunately succumbed to temptation: there are still luxury cars on the road and many unfinished building projects.

The banks' generosity stopped as soon as the crisis hit, leaving many Greeks in serious debt. The only compensation is that the banks now cannot find buyers for houses they want to auction, with the only chance of profit coming from luxury properties going for prices above one million euros. However, there is hope on the horizon: many Turkish people currently living under the Erdogan regime are looking increasingly for property on Rhodes.

BEACHES FOR EVERYONE

All of Rhodes' beaches are open to the public free of charge – although they can be state-leased for private purposes. Not all of the beaches are packed with sun loungers and parasols, and you are welcome to spread your towel out anywhere. Beach tavernas and bars line the promenades and water-sports facilities can be found in all major resorts between mid-May and mid-October. Lifeguards are a rare sight on beaches due to the lack of funding from the local councils.

BYZANTINE

You will encounter the word "Byzantine" on thousands of brown signs dotted all over Rhodes. The Byzantine era was the continuation of the Roman Empire in the East from around 500 to 1453, roughly the same period as our Middle Ages. Until 1309, Rhodes belonged to the Byzantine Empire. This Empire spread across all of Asia Minor, the Balkans and Greece. Its capital city was Constantinople, which was renamed as Istanbul when it fell to the Ottoman Turks in 1453. However, the Ecumenical Patriarch of the Eastern Orthodox Church (the equivalent of

Genuinely Byzantine: Ágios Nikólaos Fountoúkli chapel

the Catholic Pope) still resides in the city. The official flag of the Greek Orthodox Church shows a black Byzantine double-headed eagle on a yellow background; it can be seen flying in front of many churches and monasteries on Rhodes.

COLOSSAL

What a colossal man! One of the Seven Wonders of the World, cast in bronze between 294 and 282 BCE and 33 metres high, the Colossus of Rhodes stood either astride the harbour entrance or on the acropolis high above the town. Only 50 years later, it was destroyed by an earthquake. The bronze was melted down and not a single piece was preserved. However, the Colossus of Rhodes is present everywhere on the island today, with souvenirs ranging from metal statues

to prop up your book shelves to colourful postcards and sunbathing towels.

CRISIS MANAGEMENT

Krísis? What crisis? Most island inhabitants see the economic crisis, which erupted in Greece in 2009, as a chronic illness from which the country may never fully recover. Salaries, pensions and the minimum wage were all cut while taxes rose considerably. Even now, unemployment remains very high, particularly among the young.

During the crisis, the people on Rhodes adapted their lifestyle accordingly. They planted vegetables instead of ornamental shrubs, got used to only ordering what they could eat in tavernas, bought smaller cars and stopped building new houses. Today, they give each other a helping hand rather than relying on casual labour from overseas. Although the global pandemic of Covid-19 added to their woes in 2020 and 2021, the tourism sector is expected to bounce back to support the wider economy in the coming years.

EARLY EU

Around 700 years ago, something like the EU already existed – and its capital was not Brussels, but Rhodes. In the state of the Order of the Knights of St John, Christians from many European countries lived together peacefully and voted in their ruler for a lifetime. It did not matter much where you were born. Instead, everyone was organised according to "tongues", which were something like "languages" at the time.

FALSE FRIEND

Nee in Greek is a false friend for speakers of many European languages. Greeks say *nee* when they get married, for example, and it simply means "yes". The commonly used word *entáxi* is another cause for confusion. No, the Greeks don't want to travel by taxi all the time, they are simply saying "okay".

GREEN – THE COLOUR OF HOPE

Although the Greeks recognise the importance of protecting the environment, the country simply does not have the resources. With no incineration plant and thankfully no nuclear power plant, the island relies on two normal power stations, an old one near Soróni and a new one near Prassoníssi, both of which burn crude oil. Alternative forms of energy have

Irony of fate: sun god Helios, the Colossus of Rhodes, was eventually melted down

had mixed success. When a solar park developer went bankrupt, many private investors on Rhodes lost a lot of money and locals are now understandably sceptical to invest in solar parks. Wind energy is not exploited enough. The only sector where Rhodes has gained ground is in its use of solar panels. They can be seen on many hotel roofs and private residences, and show that the average citizen can make very good savings by going green.

HARPOONS

Kamáki translates literally as harpoon, but its meaning is a Casanova, and it is practically a profession in Rhodes. Adorned with gold chains and big rings, young men and older playboys try to court and conquer female tourists on holiday. They see themselves as irresistible and are organised in groups in private clubs. The *kamáki* men are unique to Rhodes, and the documentary film *Colossi of Love* reported on this phenomena. They keep a list of their successes: who managed to court the most women and the most nationalities? They are not troublesome, and they will leave anyone alone who is obviously not interested in their "services". The womanizers see themselves as athletes and stick to "fair play" rules.

IN BEST COMPANY

People on Rhodes do not like spending time on their own. A cosy twosome is reserved for a certain hour of the day. Otherwise, Greeks prefer a *paréa*: a group of friends or acquaintances who

TRUE OR FALSE?

ALL GREEKS DANCE THE SYRTÁKI

It was Hollywood star Anthony Quinn who made the Syrtáki famous around the world. Since he danced it in *Zorba the Greek*, all foreigners are convinced that it is the quintessential Greek dance. In fact, the dance was invented specifically for the film, probably because real Greek folk dances would have been a little too complicated for the US audience. In recognition of putting Greece back on the map, Anthony Quinn was presented with his own piece of land by the military rulers of Hellas at the time: "Anthony Quinn Bay" south of Faliráki. And in the areas where foreign holidaymakers flock, the simple dance remains tremendously popular. During the "get up and dance" stage of "Greek nights" in local restaurants, the Syrtáki can be counted on delivering a packed dance floor.

WE HELPED THE GREEK ECONOMY

The international efforts to save Greece from bankruptcy may have cost billions, but few Greeks felt rescued by foreign governments. People argue that the money didn't stay in Greece, but instead was handed on to foreign banks to repay the country's debt.

regularly meet up to drink coffee or eat, go to the disco and holiday together. The question asked by friends afterwards is not what the hotel or food was like, but how the *paréa* was.

In case you do have to go it alone, you will always be accompanied by the island's saints. They are present as icons wherever you go – whether in the taxi, in the ticket booth or in the open fields – either as printed images or painted on church and chapel walls and hanging on the sides of the road. You know you are always in safe hands and in good company.

KOMBOLOIA

The *Komboloi* is a set of worry beads, often carried by old men and available in souvenir shops. Although it resembles a Catholic rosary, it is a variation of Turkish prayer beads. The Greeks adopted their own style of bead for relaxation, enjoyment and generally passing the time. The *kómbos*, or knot used to hold the beads together, is regarded as a lucky charm. Apparently it also helps people to quit smoking.

LAND OF CONFUSION

People from Rhodes hate strict rules, and are quite liberal where their spelling is concerned; a custom which can confuse many a tourist. In Greek, place names can be written differently on signs and maps, while the Latin spelling is even more haphazard. *Agía* meaning "saint" is a good example. It is sometimes written as *Agía* (as in the Marco Polo guides) or *Aghía* or even

Ayía. All three spellings are accepted and combined as the Greeks please. Where there are no rules, there are fewer mistakes.

NO HURRY

Do you know what tomorrow will bring? The Rhodians certainly don't know and don't waste their time planning for the long term. Large events and festivals are only made public a few days in advance, while timetables or the opening times of museums or excavation sites are posted online at short notice.

Vague arrangements to meet the following morning, afternoon, evening or even next week are made, adding the all-important *"ta léme"* – "we'll talk again later." You can then expect a call one hour beforehand to confirm the exact time – give or take the customary half an hour.

Enjoy a drink and some shade at Elli Beach

TÁVLI

Two men sit at a table with a board, two dice and chunky plastic tokens between them, their heads bowed, muscles taut – do not disturb! *Távli* is much more than just the Greek version of backgammon. It's as much a part of the life of the traditionally minded Greek male, and many a young Greek woman, as the car keys and the mobile phone on the table. You can rent the board game in almost every café and many bars. Just Google the rules!

TECHNO VERSUS ENTECHNO

Beware of confusing the words because there is a world of difference between techno and *entechno* music, although both genres are loved by young Rhodians. *Entechno* could be translated as a "synthetic song": it describes rock ballads with Greek lyrics, mostly performed by a solo singer and accompanied by only a guitar. This music is also appreciated by people who don't like techno. At the current time, Giórgos Daláras (georgedalaras. com) and Giánnis Haroúlis are the most prominent *entechno* artists.

VISITS FROM THE NEIGHBOURS

For a long time, NATO's partner Turkey was the arch-enemy of many Greeks. Although ties improved considerably in the 1990s, the relationship has gradually deteriorated since the refugee crisis and Erdogan's threat to Turkish democracy.

This situation does not change the fact that day trippers from Turkey have been a blessing in disguise for bar and restaurant owners on Rhodes. The Turkish like to dine in style, and unlike many other tourists order far more than just a Greek salad. They also appreciate traditional Greek music and enjoy live performances, as the Eastern-influenced sounds are familiar to them. They even employ the services of an interpreter to translate the lyrics.

EATING
SHOPPING
SPORT

Al fresco dining on the terraces of Líndos

EATING & DRINKING

RETURNING TO THEIR ROOTS

Mediterranean cuisine, along French and Italian lines, is en vogue, while restaurants serving Indian, Japanese and Mexican food are competing fiercely with the established ones, especially in the island's capital. Young Greek chefs and restaurant and bar owners are holding their own by returning to the best traditional style of cooking from their grandmothers' day and giving it a creative make-over, using largely fresh, regional produce.

THE PARÉA IS WHAT MATTERS

Greeks love to have a great variety of different dishes on the table at one time. They seldom go out alone for dinner in the evening, though, as eating in company is preferable to a cosy dinner for two. The company of friends and relatives at the table, collectively known as the *paréa*, is considered to be just as important as the culinary experience. The diners always order plenty of dishes, which are placed in the centre of the table. Each person takes as much as they like of whatever they fancy. Usually there will be meat and fish served up on large platters, and everyone helps themselves. Traditionally, more food is ordered than can possibly be eaten: to eat everything is not "the done thing", as it would be a sign of obviously having ordered too little. All plates, even the empty ones, remain on the table. The waiter does not clear them away, so that everyone can see how well the *paréa* has dined.

A LITTLE BIT OF EVERYTHING, PLEASE

You can best enjoy the whole spectrum of Greek cooking if, like the locals themselves, you order a variety of starters – *mesédes* – rather than choosing a traditional menu as you

Kali orexi (enjoy your meal)! Greek starters (left) and grilled seafood (right)

would elsewhere in Europe. You can often even do without a main course. These *mesédes* include various purées and thick sauces which the Greeks designate as salads. Other favourites are croquettes made of different vegetables, also from squid, puréed fish roe and potato *(taramà)* or your common or garden chicken. The potato patties or mashed chickpeas rolled into balls are delicious. The turnovers, or *píttes*, made of puff pastry and filled with cheese and/or spinach, sausage or meat, are a traditional favourite. Fried slices of aubergine or courgettes also count as *mesédes*, as do fresh salads, pickled fish, anchovies, olives, oven-baked cheese and seafood.

LOTS OF FISH & MEAT

When it comes to main courses, Greek chefs are less imaginative. If their compatriots go out to eat they want meat and fish from the charcoal grill. Accompanying sauces are rare – at best there will be a mixture of good olive oil and lemon to go with the fish. Jacket potatoes or potatoes roasted in the oven are becoming more popular, but the usual side dishes are more or less poor cousins to standard chips. Dishes cooked in the oven are a traditional highlight in Greek cuisine. Everyone has heard of the famous casseroles topped with béchamel sauce, such as *moussaká* (aubergines and mincemeat) or *pastítsjo* (macaroni and mincemeat). Baked aubergines, lamb baked in the oven with potatoes *(kleftikó)* or lamb baked in foil with vegetables *(exochikó)* are all delicious.

FOR THOSE WITH A SWEET TOOTH

Rhodian desserts have a touch of the East about them. You'll rarely find them on the menu at a restaurant; you

An old master in the traditional art of making *kataífi*

from northern Greece, the *bougátsa* is a turnover made of strudel dough and filled either with vanilla custard or sheep's cheese.

HOT FOOD AROUND THE CLOCK

In the more traditional villages and in the towns, most tavernas are open from 9am until midnight. The Greeks eat wherever and whenever they fancy, and not when the landlord decides. Lunch is often eaten as late as 2 or 3pm, and it is common to get together with your *paréa* – your friends or relatives – 10 or 11pm.

FROM CAFFEINE TO TANNIN

The island's favourite hot beverage is coffee in its many different variations. Whether traditional mocha *(kafés ellinikós)*, instant or filter coffee espresso or cappuccino – served hot or cold – you must say how sweet you want it because the ground coffee is mixed with sugar and then brewed. You also need to order the milk separately for espresso, instant and filter coffee.

Whisky is the Greeks' favourite spirit, yet the traditional ouzo, made of aniseed, is widespread. In rural areas people like to drink *soúma*, distilled from the remains of grapes after pressing and similar to an Italian grappa. To accompany your meal, you are served water, wine or beer, which is often available on draught. Wines from the island's major wineries Cair and Emery are available everywhere. Lovers of rarer labels should ask for something from the Rhodian winery Tríantáfyllou or from Ktíma Papaioánnou and Ktíma Mércouri on the Peloponnese.

have to go instead to a *zacharoplastío*, the Greek equivalent of a cake or pastry shop. There are plenty of these, but outside Rhodes Town they seldom offer somewhere to sit down. Local residents usually take their cakes home with them. The best place to indulge your sweet tooth is to trawl around the pastry shops on the harbour side of the Néa Agorá market in Rhodes Town. The often colourful creamy cakes and gateaux are a delight to look at; however, the apple cakes *(milópitta)* and walnut cakes *(karidópitta)* are considered as more typically Greek. Both can be enjoyed with ice cream, which also goes well with the eastern-style pastries, such as *baklavás* and *kataífi*, eaten with a knife and dessert fork. Traditionally

INSIDER TIP
Sweets heaven

Today's Specials

Starters

CHORIÁTIKI SALÁTA
A mixed Greek salad with feta cheese

CHTAPÓDI KSIDÁTO
Octopus pickled in vinegar and onions

PATSÁRIA
Beetroot, mostly cooked with the leaves, but not pickled

Meat & fish

JEMISTÉS
Peppers and tomatoes filled with rice and minced meat

JUVÉTSI
Pasta that looks like grains of rice, baked in a clay dish with beef or lamb

STIFÁDO
Beef or rabbit stew in a tomato and cinnamon sauce with onions

KSIFÍA
Grilled boneless swordfish steak

Vegetarian

BRIÁM
Ratatouille with lots of aubergines and olive oil

DOLMÁDES
Stuffed vine leaves, mostly served hot in an egg and lemon sauce

FÁVA
Puréed yellow peas with onions and olive oil

REVITHÓKEFTÉDES
A purée of chickpeas shaped into patties or balls and fried

Desserts

BAKLAVÁ
A filo pastry filled with chopped nuts or almonds, also served with ice cream

HALVÁ
Confectionery made of toasted semolina with sugar syrup

RISÓGALO
A thin rice pudding with a touch of cinnamon

SHOPPING

Rhodes is a good money-saving destination. You can find a new summer outfit and fashionable accessories, or culinary specialities and the usual kitsch for your relatives to take back home. The best places to shop are in Rhodes Town and Líndos.

A COLOSSUS TO TAKE HOME
Although nobody knows what the ancient Colossus of Rhodes looked like, you will come across representations of it in souvenir shops everywhere on the island – on bathing towels, postcards, shopping bags and coasters. Of course, it is also a popular image on umbrellas (see opposite).

CERAMICS
Rhodes is an island of potters. You'll find a large number of potters' studios and showrooms on the road between Faliráki and Líndos, particularly around Archángelos. The colourful enamelled wall plates are typical of Rhodes.

CULINARY TREATS
Rhodian wine, liqueurs and Rhodian ouzo may still be transported home in your flight baggage. Pickled olives, herbs, pistachios, coffee or honey will conjure up the tastes and smells of the sunny island on your dining table.

FASHION
You can buy Versace & co. anywhere in the world – but the fashionable creations of Greek designers are sold almost exclusively in Greece, for example in Rhodes and Líndos.

LEATHER GOODS
As animal fur has become taboo in most cultures, the island's furriers have had to adapt accordingly. Many have converted to selling leather although many just import items from

You'll find everything from olive oil to a new pair of sandals in Rhodes Town

the more renowned leather-producing countries of Turkey and Italy. There is only one small workshop in the Old Town which makes its own sandals, handbags and belts.

NATURAL SPONGES

Traditional ships operate as stores for sea-sourced items from all over the world at the harbour in Emborikó Limáni, with cheap shells usually coming from the Caribbean. Natural sponges from the nearby Greek island of Kálimnos are more expensive.

SHOES

Women on Rhodes are an adventurous kind. They like their shoes to have bright colours and unusual shapes, and with heels that are murderously high. Some of these innovations may become fashionable in Central Europe a couple of years later, but the majority are only worn on Rhodes. You can

also find all kinds of sneakers, trainers and sandals. Most of the shoe shops are located in the New Town.

SOUVENIRS FROM TURKEY

Day-trippers to Turkey should be aware of the customs regulations when returning to Rhodes. The following limits apply: 40 cigarettes or 50g of tobacco, 1litre of spirits (over 22% abv) or 2 litres (under 22% abv), plus items for personal use to the value of 430 euros.

UMBRELLAS

Despite the sunshine, Rhodes is a world capital when it comes to umbrellas. Virtually no tourist leaves Rhodes without buying one. You can find all types, from a three-euro umbrella to designer pieces. Most stores are situated around the *Platía Kyprou* (see p. 53) in the New Town.

INSIDER TIP
Be prepared

SPORT & ACTIVITIES

On the search for the ultimate experience? Try horseback-riding through the Rhodian "prairie". More suited to water? Rhodes is not just a sunny island; it's windy too, offering perfect conditions for both windsurfers and kitesurfers. You can also try piloting a motorboat as you do not need to have a sailing licence. The waters around the island are not only home to fish but shipwrecks too, making them ideal for divers to explore. Mountain bikers and hikers will find routes through the unspoilt interior of the island. Some of the island's rocks are even suitable for rock climbing.

ACTIVITY HOLIDAYS

If you love a rush of adrenalin and exciting thrills, contact *Rhodes Activities Booking (tel. 69 45 99 51 68 | FB: RhodesActivitiesBooking)* who will help you organise a tour to suit your tastes; it is run by two young men, Jórgos and Stéfanos, who offer a list of activities provided by various operators on the island. They can help you book tours and even organise transfers to and from the locations. The activities available range from riding and diving, hiking and cycling, rock climbing and windsurfing (both in conjunction with yoga), stand-up paddleboarding, paintballing and paramotor flights. It's definitely worth checking out their Facebook page.

BOAT HIRE

Pedalos can be hired on many beaches *(approx. 10 euros/hr)*. On the beach at Stegná and at Faliráki harbour you can hire motor boats without having to have a licence *(from approx. 45 euros /hr)*.

CLIMBING

Rhodes is home to a small group of enthusiastic rock climbers who have

Wind? Check! Waves? Check! The island is a kitesurfer's paradise

created routes in various regions of the island: near Ladikó, Archángelos, Charáki, Líndos and Siána. If you want to try this sport, it is best to contact local climbers on Facebook *(climbing-inrhodes)* or take a look at the website *rodosclimb.gr*.

DIVING

Scuba diving is permitted on Rhodes at several marked stretches along the coast when accompanied by a licensed instructor. The dive centre run by young Greeks, *Lepia Dive Center (tel. 69 37 41 79 70 | lepiadive.com)* in Péfki and Plimmíri also accommodates disabled divers.

Several boats leave daily for dive tours from Mandráki Harbour in Rhodes Town. Even completely novice divers can take their first dip down to a depth of 5–6m. Local providers include *Waterhoppers (Odós Kritiká 45 | Rhodes Old Town | tel. 22 41 03 81 46 | waterhoppers.com)*. Dive Med *(at the Magic Life Club | Plimmíri | tel. 69 46 25 94 09 | divemed.gr)* specialises in diving excursions in the island's south and also offers snorkelling trips departing from Plimmíri harbour.

ER TIP
Immerse yourself!

HIKING

Rhodes is ideal hiking country. However, there are no proper walking maps and no signposted trails, and hiking guidebooks date quickly. If you want to see the island on foot, you are advised to book a complete hiking holiday with your local travel agency. Guided day trips can be booked with *Impress Holidays (Odós Prágas 11 | Kolímbia | tel. 22 41 06 03 72 | impressnet.gr)*.

HORSE RIDING

A dream destination for horse lovers is *Elpida Ranch (tel. 69 48 13 29 77 |*

elpidaranch.eu). A German-Rhodian couple has created a small paradise in total isolation between Laérma and the Thári Monastery. They also

INSIDER TIP
A special day on horseback

have pigs and chickens, an improvised pool, a friendly sun terrace and a small archery facility. Children can ride on ponies; more experienced riders can go on hacks that can take several days. Everything is very laid-back; it's best to call ahead and talk about a programme that suits you best.

Rather more conventional and touristy, the *Fívos Horse Riding Club (signposted on the main road | Faliráki | tel. 69 46 36 99 18 | fivos-horse-riding.com)* near Faliráki offers, among other things, 90-minute guided hacks along the beach, even for absolute beginners.

MOUNTAIN BIKING

For mountain bikers, Rhodes provides ideal terrain. There are plenty of quiet, asphalted roads in the centre of the island and countless more dirt tracks. A particularly good agency that offers guided tours is *Rodos Cycling (Apollonious Amerikis 49 | Rhodes Town | tel. 69 47 30 99 11 | rodoscycling.com). SD Bikes (Odós Kodrigktónos 69 | tel. 22 41 07 35 11 | sdbikes.gr)* and *Rhodos Bicycle Rental (Odós Th. Sofoúli 97 | tel. 22 41 02 12 64 | rhodosbicyclerental. gr)* are also situated in Rhodes New Town. On the west coast, *Impress Holidays (Odós Prágas 11 | Kolímbia | tel. 22 41 06 03 72 | impressnet.gr)* offer guided tours and rental bikes.

WATER SPORTS

A variety of water sports are on offer on almost all beaches adjoining the larger hotels. You can go windsurfing, parasailing, waterskiing or sea canoeing, or you can hire a pedalo, a canoe or a paddleboard.

The well-protected bay at Líndos is well suited to waterskiing. Stand-up paddleboarding is the specialty of *Paddle Paradise (90-minute course 35 euros, 3- to 4-hour guided tour 59 euros | in front of the Limnióni taverna | Stegná Beach | te.*

Take part in a variety of activities by, in or on the water, such as here in Stegná

69 81 56 87 98 | paddleparadise.gr).

An ideal spot for experienced windsurfers is the beach at Prassoníssi in the far south of the island. Wind and kitesurfers like the beaches between Ixiá and Theológos on the west coast the best. There are some busy kite stations in Fánes *(kite-rhodos.com, meltemi-kiteclub.com).*

A good water-sports station is the *Kiotári Watersports Centre (surfing course: 10hrs approx. 180 euros | on the beach in front of the hotels Rodos Maris and Rodos Princess | Kiotári | tel.* *22 44 02 32 79 | watersports-rhodes. com).* Here you can go surfing or get your catamaran sailing licence *(6-8 hrs incl. exam fees: 280 euros)* or windsurfing licence from the International School Association for Water Sports (VDWS).

In the north of the island in Ixiá is *Windsurfers' World (tel. 22 41 02 49 95 | windsurfersworld.gr)*, a good centre which also runs a *Kite Pro Center* in Kremastí *(kiteprocenter.gr)*. Prices and sports on offer are similar to those of Kiotári Watersports Centre.

M e d i t e r r a n e a n

S e a

Popular bathing resorts, extensive forest and unspoilt countryside

Kritinía

Ér

Emborió

Monólithos

LÍNDOS &

Kattavía

10 km
6.21 mi

Countless sights to visit, tavernas, shops and even a beach

Ródos

Ialisós

RHODES TOWN **p. 38**

Kalithiés

E CENTRE **p. 80**

Arhángelos

SOUTH **p. 58**

Líndos

tári

The beauty queen of the Aegean Sea, plus quiet villages and long beaches

M e d i t e r r a n e a n

S e a

RHODES TOWN

A UNIQUE CITY

There may be more beautiful cities in the world but none that have such a well-preserved and extensive medieval core. After 2,400 years of uninterrupted settlement, Rhodes Old Town is alive with history. Mosques and minarets, churches and a synagogue show that multiculturalism is not a modern invention; and the 2,000-year-old remains are testimony to monumental architectural achievement in a period when most other Europeans were still living in caves and huts.

The old and the new coexist in the island's capital

Buildings dating from half a millennia ago are now small boutique hotels, bars and tavernas. The streets of the Old Town resemble a bustling bazaar, while the side lanes are populated by more cats than people. Countless yachts are moored in beautiful Mandráki Harbour, while fishing boats and cruise liners dock in front of the mighty city walls. The New Town, with its modern shops and hotels, stretches along two beaches; this is where tourists come to party while young Greeks prefer to chill out in the Old Town until sunrise.

RHODES TOWN

MARCO POLO HIGHLIGHTS

★ **OLD TOWN**
Every stone and every building within the medieval city walls is worth a look ➤ p. 42

★ **MUSEUM OF ARCHAEOLOGY**
Ancient treasures displayed in an old medieval hospital ➤ p. 42

★ **AVENUE OF THE KNIGHTS**
Follow the cobbled street back to Crusader times ➤ p. 44

★ **PALACE OF THE GRAND MASTER**
Quite a sight – whichever way you look at it ➤ p. 44

★ **ODÓS SOKRATOÚS**
Named after the famous philosopher, this street in the Old Town is lined with interesting stores ➤ p. 45

★ **MANDRÁKI HARBOUR**
The finest harbour on the entire island ➤ p. 46

★ **NÉA AGORÁ**
Get together at the market hall at any time of the day ➤ p. 47

★ **FILÉRIMOS**
With ancient ruins and a romantic monastery , this mountain offers a bird's-eye view of Rhodes ➤ p. 55

★ **KALLITHÉA SPRINGS**
Splash around in the historic ambience of these unique thermal springs ➤ p. 56

200 m
219 yd

Elli Beach

Elli Beach

Mediterranean

Sea

Casino

N. Savva

G. Papanikolaou

Kathopouli

I. Efstathiou

Hatjantonis

Amerikis

25 Martiou

D. Themeli

Gr. Lambraki

Makariou

Ethnarchou

15 Turkish Cemetery

7 Martiou

Dodekanison

Εθνάρχου Μακαρίου

Gallias

Γαλλίας

Karpathou

Averof

ΑΛ. Παπάγου

Al. Papagou

14 Promenade

12 Mandráki Harbour ★

Aktaíon

Platía Kyprou

Blanc du Nil

13 Néa Agorá ★

Kontiki Next

Akti Maoumpoulinas

2 City walls and moat

16 Museum of Modern Greek Art

the Grand Master ★ **5**

Avenue of the Knights ★ 4

Orfeos

Pisandrou

Ippoton

Lachitos

Clock tower **6**

Mama Sofia

Kamíros

Socratous Garden

Kaberis

3 Museum of Archaeology ★

Dinóris

Ibiscus

7 Odós Sokratoús ★

Haris Cotton

1 Old Town ★

Ακτή Σαχτούρη

Akti Sachtouri

Akti Sachtouri

Akti Promitheos

Platía Ariónos **8**

Fanouriou

Aghiou

Platonos

Soleskous

Lysippou

Pindarou

Dimosthenous

Ikarou

Thiseos

Gavala

☑ 11 Kahal Shalom Synagogue

Ágios Fanoúrios **9**

Ippodamou

Iosifou

Omirou

Walk Inn

10 Platía Doriéos

Aristidou

Pythagora

Solokleous

Perikleous

Tavisiou

Kisthiniou

Kallithéa Springs ★

dini Park

Dimokratias

Aegean Fish

WHERE TO START?

Ideally, visit the capital by bus or taxi, since parking spaces are rare. The bus station is directly behind the **Néa Agorá**, just a few steps from the Old Town and Mandráki Harbour. If you do decide to go by car, you're most likely to find a reasonably priced parking space between Mandráki Harbour, the Town Hall and the Aquarium.

SIGHTSEEING

1 OLD TOWN ★

The Old Town of Rhodes is a UNESCO World Heritage Site that catapults you back 2,500 years into history. It is impossible to lose your way: the old city is fully enclosed by its 4-km-long *city wall*. You can either walk on top of the wall or within its 2.5-km-long *moat* which skirts the city inland.

The best way to get your bearings around the Old Town is to follow the main streets, and then explore the quieter corners by walking in a zigzag direction. Buildings erected by the Byzantines, Crusaders, Israelites, Ottoman Turks and Greeks are embedded in the ancient fortifications; there are no new constructions spoiling the view.

Despite its antiquity, holidaymakers from around the world give this city its cosmopolitan flair. It's also fun to watch the world strut its stuff along the cobblestone catwalks in front of the many street cafés and tavernas. *a–f 1–6*

2 CITY WALLS & MOAT

Towering over the city's harbour, the fortifications of Rhodes were undeniably an intimidating sight to the Turkish soldiers who invaded in 1522. Their mission to conquer the city probably seemed downright impossible. Indeed, the siege lasted six months and the besiegers had to resort to starving the city's inhabitants. The knights finally surrendered and withdrew from the island.

A stroll through the deep, very wide 🐖 moat will give you an impression of the colossal task facing the Ottoman invaders *(main entrances on the Platía Riminis c4 and the Pylí Arkadía e5 | freely accessible).* Try for fun just lifting one of the many stone cannon balls that are lying around. For a change of perspective, climb up onto the city walls *(April–Oct Mon–Fri 10am–3pm | admission 2 euros; tickets at the Palace of the Grand Master)* and look down into the moat. Dizzying! Sturdy shoes and surefootedness are essential if you want to walk along the accessible part of the 4-km-long wall. Your reward: a great view over the roofs and minarets of the Old Town, which was declared a UNESCO World Heritage Site in 1988. ⊘ *30–60 mins | a–f 2–6*

INSIDER TIP
How strong are you?

3 MUSEUM OF ARCHAEOLOGY ★

The island's most significant museum lures even the most reluctant visitor to spend more than an hour inside because it is far more than just an

If you are surefooted and not scared of heights, climb on to the city walls

exhibition space. Surrounded by beautiful gardens and overlooking a large courtyard with a pile of cannon balls and an ancient marble lion, the two-storey building itself is a perfect photo opportunity. Its finest treasure is a small marble Aphrodite statue depicting the goddess with a beautifully sculpted figure. However, the tour begins by following the 28-step open staircase up to the first-floor arcade. Walk through the largest doorway to enter a long, high-ceilinged room that dates back to the 15th century: the sick and the injured were treated in this room by the Knights of Saint John when the building served as a hospital. The gravestones on the wall are in memory of those who couldn't be saved. A small door leads into the dining halls where two Aphrodite statues stand. There you will also find a tomb stele heralded as a masterpiece of Greek classicism; dating from around 410 BCE, the stele depicts Krito and Timarista: a young woman mourning the loss of her dead mother.

Continue along a terrace with more sculptures and out into the gardens, where beautiful ancient mosaics are exhibited in an open-air foyer. One of the mosaics depicts a centaur (half horse, half man) returning from the hunt with its prey, a scrawny looking rabbit, hanging from its mouth. From the gardens, visitors can visit two other special exhibitions concentrating on Rhodes in the Minoan and Mycenaean period in the 2nd millennium BCE. Stairs lead up to the upper arcade to 12 side rooms which mainly hold painted ceramics found in Rhodes dating between 500 BCE and 500 CE.

When you leave the museum and turn left, you reach another museum room which is only accessible from the street. This space showcases enormous pottery vessels once used to bury the dead in a squatting position – they couldn't have found it too uncomfortable. *Easter–Oct daily 8am–8pm, Nov–Easter Tue–Sun 8am–2.40pm; special exhibitions April–Oct only daily 9am–4.50pm | admission 4 euros | Odós Apéllou | Old Town | ⏱ 1–2 hrs | 🗺 c3*

4 AVENUE OF THE KNIGHTS ★

Odós Ippotón is the only late medieval residential street in Europe that has remained fully intact. It runs in a perfectly straight line from the hospital of the Order of St John, which now houses the Museum of Archaeology,

Antique mosaics in the Palace of the Grand Master

to the Palace of the Grand Master. To the left and right stand the inns of the various "tongues" of the Order (see "Early EU", p. 18), decorated with the heraldic emblems of each Grand Master. The finest emblem belonged to the French knights and stands almost in the centre. *Permanently accessible; building interiors cannot be viewed | Odós Ippotón | Old Town | 🗺 b–c3*

5 PALACE OF THE GRAND MASTER ★ 🛈

The most photographed and visited sight in the Old Town is, in fact, a fake. The Italians reconstructed the Palace of the Grand Master of the Knights of Rhodes in the early 1930s to suit the tastes of the megalomaniac dictator Mussolini. It was planned to be his residence if he ever came to live on the island, but he was too busy masterminding wars so stayed in Rome.

In 1856, a bolt of lightning triggered an explosion that blew up the church and turned the original palace into a mass of ruins. Only a few parts of the original structure remain, including the monumental entrance portal with its impressive towers. The building's interior was completely redesigned with ancient mosaics from the island of Kos, solid wood furnishings and Chinese porcelain – elements unknown to the Order of the Knights of St John, whose Grand Master resided here from the late 14th century to 1522. The building lost its importance when the Turks invaded; they used the hospital as an army barracks and prison, the palace's church as a cowshed, and the neighbouring church of the Order as an arsenal.

The ground floor hosts two exhibitions. From a historical perspective, these exhibits are far more valuable than the actual building. One is dedicated to Byzantine Rhodes from the fourth century to 1522. The second, more interesting, exhibit is "Rhodes 2400", showcasing recent archaeological findings. Because archaeologists tend to dig faster than they write, many of these sensational objects have not yet been listed, and therefore cannot be photographed, nor can you buy postcards of them. *April–Oct daily 8am–8pm, Nov–March Tue–Sun 8.30am–2.40pm; special exhibitions April–Oct only, daily 9am–4.40pm | admission April–Oct 6 euros, Nov–March 3 euros | Platía Kleovoúlou | ☉ 2–3 hrs | ⊞ b2*

Navigation aids: the clock tower and the minaret of the Mosque of Suleiman

6 CLOCK TOWER

It is well worth climbing the clock tower to take in the fabulous view over the roofs and towers of the Old Town. *May–Oct daily 9am–11pm | admission (incl. a refreshing drink) 5 euros | Odós Orféos 1 | Old Town | ☉ 10 mins | ⊞ b3*

7 ODÓS SOKRATOÚS (SOCRATES STREET) ★

Shopping is on the agenda when you arrive at Socrates Street, the main street running through the Old Town. The street climbs gently uphill from Platía Ippokrátous at the bottom to the Mosque of Suleiman at the top. The street is lined on both sides with shops selling all the usual souvenirs and

more: jewellery and freshly roasted coffee, leather and furs, natural cosmetics and Greek culinary specialities, kitsch, t-shirts and even lightweight suits of armour. Standing at a slight angle halfway down the street is the tiny *Mehmet Aga Mosque. Bekersir (no. 76)*, the island's oldest coffee house where

INSIDER TIP
Have a puff

you may want to try a traditional hookah, stands diagonally opposite the mosque.

From here, head up the street to the pink-coloured *Mosque of Suleiman* at the top end. Dating from the 19th century, the mosque no longer holds acts of worships *(not open to the public)*. Opposite is the tiny *Turkish Library (April–Oct Mon–Sat 9am–3pm | free admission | ☉ 10 mins)* built in the

18th century. The library contains Turkish, Persian and Arabic manuscripts and books depicting Islamic culture. *□ b-d 3-4*

8 PLATÍA ARIÓNOS

This tiny square with a mosque and large Turkish baths was a hive of activity in Ottoman times. Today the square is frequented mainly by locals who come in the evenings to relax in the three music cafés. *Old Town | □ b4*

9 ÁGIOS FANOÚRIOS

INSIDER TIP
Saintly assistance

Have you forgotten or lost something? Greeks in this case call on the help of Saint Fanoúrios. According to many devout followers, he works better than any lost property office. The ancient church in the city is dedicated to this patron saint of lost belongings and has its origins in the ninth century. This antiquity can be seen clearly below the ground level of the present structure, which dates back to the Crusader period. Between the sooty frescoes from the 13th to 15th century, you can well imagine how people used to gather here in candlelight. *Open in the daytime | Odós Agíou Fanoúriou | ⊙ 10–15 mins | □ c5*

10 PLATÍA DORIÉOS

Three bars and a minaret can be found on this square. The bars serve mainly salads, burgers and pizzas with views of the *Rejab Pasha Mosque*, which has been waiting over 15 years for a renovation. This is a perfect place for a light lunch break. *Old Town | □ c5*

11 KAHAL SHALOM SYNAGOGUE ⚑

The synagogue, built in 1577 and destroyed by the Germans in 1943, has been renovated and now functions as a Jewish museum and place of worship open to visitors of all religions. Members of the remaining Jewish community are on hand to answer questions. *May–Oct Sun–Fri 10am–3pm | free admission | Odós Dosiádou | ⊙ 15–30 mins | □ e5*

12 MANDRÁKI HARBOUR ★

The question on everyone's lips is "Where did the famous Colossus of Rhodes once stand?" Nobody knows for sure. Legend would have you believe it stood astride the entrance to Mandráki Harbour, precisely where two pillars are now erected carrying the island's heraldic animals the stag and the doe, *elafós* and *elafína*

Whatever you're looking for, you'll probably find it at beautiful Mandráki Harbour

Mandráki is the central hub of the city. Where's the tourist information office? Mandráki. Where's the market? Mandráki. Where do the boats depart from? Mandráki. Translated into English, Mandráki means "small sheepfold". No one knows exactly how the ancient military port of Rhodes Town got its current name. One possible explanation is that the name could have something to do with its physical structure: Mandráki Harbour resembles a pair of pincers and encircles the ships rather like a fold does a herd of sheep. It's well worth a stroll around this picturesque harbour: the jetty with its three windmills and the harbour fortress *Ágios Nikólaos* all date from the 15th century. *c1*

3 NÉA AGORÁ ★ ☂

You cannot overlook this building: it has seven corners, but is only one-and-a-half storeys high. Under the arcades facing the harbour, there are a number of cafés that are busy late into night. Here, you'll find sweets such as *baklavás* and *kataífi*, originally from Turkey and now extremely popular on Rhodes. Two kiosks between the cafés sell international newspapers and magazines.

Inside the Néa Agorá stands the former fish-market hall, recognisable only by the fine fish reliefs on the capitals of its columns. Two *kafenía* and several grill restaurants are much in demand, particularly during the day. *Platía Eleftherías Mandráki | b–c1*

14 PROMENADE

The city's ample promenade is called *Eleftherías*, meaning "freedom". Its splendour and beauty unfortunately owe much to the Italian fascists who ruled over the island from 1912 to

1943, and whose architectural legacy is still evident today. They erected many classical buildings, including the Bank of Greece, the Post Office, the Harbour Master's Office, the Town Hall and the city theatre inside the fortifications, and the Governor's Palace and Bishop's Palace facing the sea. They were also responsible for the construction of the Orthodox Evangelismós church *(daily 7am–noon and 5–7.30pm | ⏱ 10 mins)*. Formerly the main church of the Knights of St John, it was reconstructed in 1925 according to old drawings, and its large walls inside are painted in traditional Byzantine style. 🗺 0

On Monte Smith: a small acropolis with a big view

15 TURKISH CEMETERY

It may seem like an unlikely place to relax and unwind, but the city's old Turkish cemetery is a perfect retreat. An old Muslim woman, whose children have left the island to work in Turkey, looks after the forlorn cemetery and is always pleased to receive a small donation. The cemetery is in the shady grounds of the tiny *Mosque of Murad Reis*, where the trees offer a perfect spot to lie down and rest for a while *Accessible during the day | access from the Platía Koundourióti | New Town | ⏱ 15–30 mins (unless you fall asleep) | 🗺 0*

16 MUSEUM OF MODERN GREEK ART

In the *Art Gallery (Platía Símis 2 | 🗺 c2)* and in the *New Art Gallery (Platía Charitou | both Tue–Sat 9am–2pm | 🗺 0)* there are displays of Greek art from the 19th and 20th centuries. Rhodes has yet to produce any masters *Admission 3 euros, valid for both exhibitions | ⏱ 20–30 mins per gallery*

🔟 AQUARIUM

The delicate proportions of the pavilion make you think of an Art Nouveau café rather than a marine biology institute. The basement of the building accommodates, apart from a marine biology museum, the aquarium tanks that are home to fish and other sea creatures from Greek waters, for example, bream, bass, prickly scorpion fish, sea urchin and starfish. *April–Oct daily 9am–8.30pm, March until 4.30pm | admission 5.50 euros | Kalímnou Lérou | hcmr.gr | ⏱ 20 mins | ▥ 0*

🔢 MONTE SMITH

Like every Greek city with its origins in antiquity, Rhodes Town has its own Acropolis. Unfortunately, little remains of its temples. Three-and-a-half columns of a temple dedicated to Apollo make up the sparse remains. A visit to the 110-m-tall hill is still worthwhile, however, as you can view the entire town from above: old and new, beautiful and ugly. Its present, rather incongruous name comes from the commander of the British fleet which was stationed on Rhodes in the early 19th century. The Italians later gave the hill the name *Monte Santo Stefano*, which is still occasionally used today. It lies in the west of the town and can be reached easily by bus. A reconstructed theatre and a partially rebuilt 🎭 stadium are also waiting to be explored. The track is exactly 201m long, and dates back to the second century BCE; it was almost completely reconstructed by the Italians, so how about a sprint? *Permanently accessible via Odós Voríou Ipírou (New Town) | bus No. 5 from Mandráki/Néa Agorá | ▥ H5*

🔟 RODINI PARK 🎭

The "green lung" of Rhodes Town lies between Monte Smith and the road to Líndos. Above the square, on a plateau, you can see a number of tombs cut into the rock face. Visitors to Greece in the 19th century named the finest one "The Tomb of the Ptolemies"; the locals call it *koúfio vounó*, the "hollow mountain". *Freely accessible during the day | get there via Odós Stéfanou Kasoúli or by bus No. 3 from Mandráki | ▥ H5*

EATING & DRINKING

AEGEAN FISH 🐷

This taverna by the weekly market serves wonderful fish at very reasonable prices. Choose your fish at the market stall and have it fried or grilled at takeaway prices. Then select side dishes and salads at the excellent self-service buffet and enjoy your food at the tables – beer garden-style. *Mon–Sat 11am–4pm | Odós Klavdíou Pepper 1 | on the road to Kallithéa | ▥ 0*

AKTAÍON 🍴 🎭

Housed in the former casino for Italian officers, this café-restaurant with its tree-shaded terrace is publicly-owned by the town and is the meeting place of cultured local clientele. The location also attracts families with young children due to the childcare facilities in the bouncy castle next door. It has a large selection of cakes to choose from

INSIDER TIP
An hour to yourself

and its tasty dishes are served in large portions. Prices are moderate, since the café depends on its regular customers. *Open daily | Platía Eleftherías | New Town | tel. 22 41 07 30 55 | €€ | ⬚ 0*

DINÓRIS
The restaurant specialises in fish and seafood. An additional bonus is that at Dinóris you dine in a lovely historic building dating to around 1300, in a hall that once served as a stable for the knights' steeds. Two specials with fish and a glass of wine are offered at lunchtime at a good price. *Open daily | Platía Mousío 14a | Old Town | tel. 22 41 02 58 24 | dinoris.com | €€€ | ⬚ c3*

KONTIKI NEXT
Relaxation for your body and soul on board the Kontiki, a classy, two-storey floating restaurant located in the Mandráki Harbour. Enjoy a coffee, ice cream, sundowner or dinner accompanied by the sounds of waves on the Mediterranean. The food is inspired by Mediterranean and Japanese cooking, with both eel and urchins on the menu. The view past the ship's mast to the fortifications, Palace of the Grand Master and Néa Agorá is spectacular. *Open daily | New Town | tel. 22 41 03 08 26 | FB: kontikinext360 | €€€ | ⬚ c1*

KOÚKOS
This multi-faceted café-restaurant is also a pub with live music. It looks a bit like the set of a Greek film, with its differently decorated areas. It offers a

variety of food at reasonable prices. Open year-round, this restaurant also has its own bakery where you can buy baked goods to take away. *Open daily | Odós Mandilára 20 | New Town | tel. 22 41 07 30 22 | €€ | ⬚ 0*

MAMA SOFIA ⚑
Mama Sofia, who opened this restaurant in 1967, is still running the eatery and arrives at 6am every day to prepare the food. At 4pm she leaves the business in the hands of her two sons Stávros and Giánnis, and Alex from Albania. Together, they provide excellent and entertaining service as well as delicious food, including succulent steaks, fish and seafood. They also serve a delicacy: *foúskes* or sea squirts. Order one to try it, but one may well be enough! The restaurant also has a small, exclusive wine cellar where wine connoisseur Stávros pours out 120 different wines by the glass. He even has bottles of the very exclusive Greek Traminer and Gewürztraminer in his cellar. *9am–11.30pm | Odós Orféos 28 | Old Town | tel. 22 41 02 44 69 | mamasofia.gr | €€ | ⬚ b3*

INSIDER TIP
Are you brave enough?

SOCRATOUS GARDEN
Enjoy a relaxing break under palm trees in this splendid garden with its own parrot in the middle of the Old Town. An ideal stopover between all the centuries, for an ice cream or drink served by a friendly, efficient staff. *Open daily | Odós Sokratoús 124 | Old Town | tel. 22 41 02 01 53 | €€ | ⬚ b3*

Socrates Street in the Old Town is perfect for strolling and people-watching

TA MARASIA

This rustic taverna attracts virtually no tourists – but the owner entices his regular customers with freshly made salads, fish and seafood. Their *fáva*

Fishy favourite (pureed chickpeas) with caramelised salmon is absolutely delicious! *Daily from 7pm | Odós Agíou Iánnou 155 | tel. 22 41 03 07 45 | €€ | ⊞ 0*

WALK INN

This modern, pub-like restaurant is frequented all year round by cosmopolitan Rhodians and foreigners living on the island. The pizzas and burgers are excellent, and changing Greek specialities from the kitchen are advertised on the chalkboard. On Sunday afternoons and evenings, you can sometimes listen to live music, from Greek Rembetiko to rock 'n' roll.

Open daily | Platía Doriéos 1 | Old Town | tel. 22 41 07 42 93 | € | ⊞ c5

SHOPPING

BLANC DU NIL

For fans of light, flowing fabrics, this French fashion company, also known as the all-white clothing store, has two stores in the city where you will find an array of white, 100 per cent Egyptian cotton clothing for men and women. *Néa Ágora | near the bus terminal | New Town | ⊞ b1* and *Odós Pindárou/ Odós Alchadef | Old Town | ⊞ e4*

HARIS COTTON

The Athenian designer team of Haris and Eva present two new collections for men and women every year made from cotton and linen. Matching accessories are also provided. *Platía Ippókratous and Odós Sokratoús 61 |*

Have you seen enough of the town and its museums? Elli Beach and the sea are nearby!

Old Town | hariscotton.gr | 🕮 d4 and c4

IBISCUS 😊
A children's dream: this shop has everything you need to feel like a real knight – from swords and battleaxes to full armour. *Odós Sokratoús 114 | Old Town | 🕮 b3*

JACOB HATJANTONIS
This shop is full of unique creations at very reasonable prices. Jacob Hatjantonis is a passionate artist who paints sandals, belts, handbags and pebbles he collects from the beach. He finds his new life much more fulfilling than his former job as a food engineer in a world-famous brewery. *Odós Mandilára 20–22 | New Town | 🕮 0*

KABERIS
Have you acquired a taste for authentic Greek coffee? You can buy a pack of freshly ground beans in this tiny coffee roastery to take back home. *Odós Sokratoús 77 | Old Town | 🕮 c4*

KAMÍROS
Are you looking for leather goods made directly on the island instead of imports from China? Then visit Níkos and Vassílis, who make everything from belts and handbags to sandals in their own shop; they also keep hind leather in their workshop. The shop even has hand-crafted leads which can be personalised. *Odós Sokratoús 175 | Old Town | 🕮 b4*

INSIDER TIP
Souvenirs f
dog owner

PLATÍA KYPROU 🛍

This tiny square abounds with boutiques selling international fashion labels, such as Paul & Shark, Trussardi, Oysho, Versace, Armani, Migato, Diesel and many others. It also has the largest selection of umbrellas in southern Europe. People always wonder why so many umbrellas are sold on an island that sees so much sunny weather. The answer lies in the past when the island was given special tax concessions and umbrellas were far cheaper here than elsewhere. You can also buy a piece of hand luggage to transport your purchases back home. *New Town | ⌘ b1*

SPORT & ACTIVITIES

SEGWAY TOURS

If nothing can throw you off balance, jump on a Segway to explore the Old Town. These two-wheel, self-balancing scooters can transport you around the cobbled streets of the city. Escorted by a guide, you can go on a two-hour tour by day or a three-hour tour by night. *59 euros/2 hrs, 85 euros/3 hrs | Ippodamou 37 | Old Town | tel. 22 41 11 24 09 | rhodesbysegway. com | ⌘ d4*

BEACHES

The city's beaches are not quiet, off-the-beaten track places. Stretching 4km along the coast, 🏖 *Elli Beach (⌘ 0)* is the closest beach to Rhodes Town and is located between Mandráki and the Aquarium. The nearest bar is always just a stone's throw away, as is

the water's edge. A 3-m-high diving platform is just 20m from the promenade. Paragliders can be spotted gliding over the bay, while the sea is full of paddle boats and waterskiers. The pebbly beach between the aquarium and airport is an alternative on less windy days.

Bathing boats leave Mandráki Harbour for the beaches along the east coast and down to Líndos; or you can reach many of the island's other beaches by bus from Néa Agorá. This makes the island's capital the perfect base for your holiday.

WELLNESS

ÁNESIS

Would you like a massage? This professional salon is frequented by local people. *Daily from 10am–9pm | from approx. 28 euros/hr | Odós Al. Diákou 65–67 | New Town | tel. 22 41 02 03 02 | FB: Anesis-Massage | ⌘ 0*

MAGÍA FISH SPA

You can get sore feet walking around Rhodes Town. In the Magía Fish Spa, more than 100 small fish nibble at your hard skin, thereby rejuvenating your feet. *Daily 9am–midnight | 10 euros for 30 mins | Odós Orféos 20 | Old Town | tel. 22 41 03 50 04 | https://magia-fish-spa.business.site | ⌘ b3*

ENTERTAINMENT

Greeks will only frequent the discos and clubs in Faliráki and other holiday resorts if they want to socialise with an international crowd. The hotel quarter in the New Town between the streets *28is Oktovríou* and *Georgíou Papanikóla* caters entirely to the whims of tourists. Greek locals prefer to hang out in the Old Town in the evenings, especially in the tiny district between the Ibrahim Pasha Mosque and Platía Ippokrátous (*d4*). After midnight, these narrow streets vibrate with sounds coming from the small bars and intimate clubs which also organise live performances. A smaller crowd also gathers at the *Platía Ariónos* in front of the former Turkish Baths.

CASINO

Even James Bond would take his dates to the casino in Rhodes Town. The building, which was constructed by the Italian fascists as *Hotel Grande Albergo delle Rose*, looks like a palace. Admission is free and you are not under any obligation to bet. Those who dare and win can take one of the casino's luxury suites, including their very own butler. *Gambling tables Mon–Thu 5pm–4am, open continuously from Fri noon until Mon 6am | slot machine casino 24/7 | minimum age 21 | admission 6 euros, tickets are valid for 7 days | Odós Georgiou Papanikolaou 4 | New Town | casinorodos.gr | O*

COLORADO

The place to let your hair down. Locals gather here to watch the live performances. The venue often plays Greek rock. *Daily from 10.30pm | tickets for live events approx. 10–15 euros incl. the first drink | Odós Orfanídou 57 | New Town | colorado.com.gr | O*

AROUND RHODES TOWN

KRÍTIKA

5km from Rhodes Town / 10 mins by bus

It's not worth a stop, but the single-storey houses lining the coastal road from the airport to the city stand empty and beg the question what they were originally built for. A tiny mosque provides a clue: when the Turks relinquished their power over Crete in 1898, several hundred Muslims moved to the Ottoman-ruled Rhodes and built the town of Krítika Their descendants later emigrated to Turkey, but the houses still belong to them. *H5*

IXIÁ

6km from Rhodes Town / 10 mins by bus

If high-rise buildings and gigantic concrete blocks of apartments do not appeal to you, then the west coast resort of Ixiá next to Faliráki is not your kind of place. This is a popular destination for package-tour holiday makers, as well as windsurfers who come for the excellent surfing conditions (see p. 35). *G5*

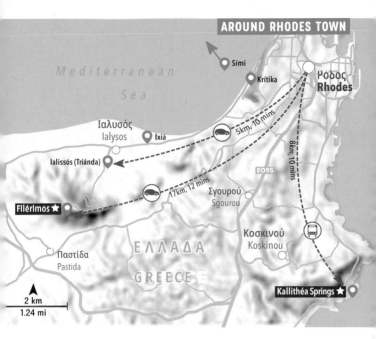

AROUND RHODES TOWN

Σίμι
Σími

Κρίτικα
Krítika

Ροδος
Rhodes

Ιαλυσός
Ialysos

Ιχiά
Ixiá

5km, 10 mins

Ιalissós (Triánda)

8km, 10 mins

EO95

17km, 12 mins

Σγουρού
Sgourou

Filérimos ★

ΕΛΛΑΔΑ

Παστίδα
Pastida

GREECE

Κοσκινού
Koskinou

2 km
1.24 mi

Kallithéa Springs ★

IALISSÓS (TRIÁNDA)
10km from Rhodes Town / 15 mins by bus

Three tourist resorts merged into one: with over 11,000 inhabitants, Triánda also known as Ialissós, is not only the island's second largest resort, but merges with its neighbours *Ixiá* and *Kremastí* to form the tourist centre of the west coast.

If you like quaint churches, have a look inside the *Kímisis tis Theotókou Church* in the village centre. It is entirely adorned with well-preserved murals in the traditional Byzantine style. The panels of the iconostasis, which separates the aisle from the altar space, are decorated with sea-horses and bare-breasted mermaids.
山 G5

FILÉRIMOS ★
17km from Rhodes Town / 15 mins by car, bus connection only in summer; 5km from Ialissós (Triánda)

Do you have a head for heights? Then drive up the 267-m-tall Filérimos Hill where you can spend a good hour admiring the view from its plateau at the top. You will find yourself in another world, surrounded by the smells of herbs and the shrill buzzing of cicadas in the pine trees and towering cypress trees.

Restored by the Italians in the 1930s, the tenth century *monastery* is a truly romantic setting, and is popular as a wedding location among local couples. Nestled in green countryside stand the scant remains of the acropolis belonging to the ancient city of

Peach, vanilla, lemon: Sími's pretty ice-cream-coloured waterfront

Ialissós, the ruins of a tiny temple dedicated to the Goddess Athena from the third or second centuries BCE. The foundations of an early Christian basilica and several chapels have also been preserved. Easily overlooked at first, the small church of *Geórgios Chostós* (Saint George) is set back into the slope; the medieval frescoes inside appear to depict kneeling knights and the eight-point cross of the Knights of St John.

Follow the alley lined with cypress trees to a viewing platform with a cross from where you are treated to the sight of planes landing and taking off at the nearby airport and a far-reaching view along Rhodes' west coast. As a souvenir, buy a miniature bottle of the herbal liquor Sette Erbe which the monks have been distilling here for centuries. *Excavation sites: April–Oct daily 8am–8pm, Nov–March Tue–Sun 8.30am–3pm |*

admission 6 euros, Nov–March 3 euros | the other paths are freely accessible | ⏱ *1–2 hrs |* ▥ *G5*

KALLITHÉA SPRINGS ★

8km from Rhodes Town / 15 mins by bus

Bathe differently: no sand, no beach. This fjord-like bay with gently sloping rock banks offers an alternative destination for sunbathing and swimming with its relaxing beach bars and sun loungers beneath palm trees, pine trees and parasols. But what catches the eye is the oriental-style dome of the art deco spa building, constructed under Italian rule, where people still come to experience the famed benefits of Kallithéa's thermal waters. Make sure that you arrive early because the spa fills up very quickly. *May–Oct daily*

INSIDER TIP
The early b

8am–8pm, Nov–April daily 8am–4pm | admission 4 euros, Nov–April 2 euros, free access to the beach bar after 8pm | kallitheasprings.gr | 🕮 H6

SÍMI

45km from Rhodes Town / 50 mins by catamaran

What an amazing sight! Tourists grab their smartphones and cameras as soon as the ship glides around the cliffs into the harbour of Sími. All three sides of the bay are covered in pastel-coloured houses spilling down the rocky coast. Overlooking the harbour is an elaborate bell tower which crowns the beauty of this idyllic village. At a time when all over Greece picturesque old buildings were torn down for the sake of "progress" to be replaced by faceless concrete blocks, the 2,600 inhabitants of the island of Sími decided instead to renovate their old houses or build new ones in the traditional style. The islanders are reaping the rewards of this wise move to this day: Sími rates as one of the most beautiful islands in the Aegean. In high season, there is a constant stream of boats arriving between 11am and 3pm.

Sími's attractions include the large monastery at *Panormítis*, the upper part of the main village which offers a very beautiful view of the harbour and the small beach at *Pédi*. Should you decide spontaneously to stay overnight, you need only inform the personnel on the ship and ask in one of the hotels or travel agencies at the harbour about a room. The food at the traditional taverna *Diethnés (tel. 22 45*

07 16 74 | €) near the bridge is also good. *Daily boats from Mandráki Harbour, no need to book in advance; ferries and catamarans operate several times per day | 🕮 0*

GREAT PLACES TO STAY

SLEEP LIKE A KNIGHT

You won't meet legendary King Arthur in the *Avalon* in Rhodes *(Old Town | Odós Charitos 9 | tel. 22 41 03 14 38 | avalonrhodes.gr | 6 rooms | €€€)*, but you are staying very near the Avenue of the Knights. The quiet courtyard, where breakfast is served, is enclosed by six suites, all of which measure at least 35m² and come with their own terrace. Owner Déspina has excellent taste and decorated the hotel herself. A caddy is available to transport your luggage from the taxi.

ONTO THE WALLS

Small and cosy: the *Cava d'Oro (Odós Kistiníou 15 | tel. 22 41 03 69 80 | cavadoro.com | 13 rooms | €€)* is the only hotel on the island with private access to the city walls. Breakfast is served in the small courtyard which borders the city wall. The 700-year old house is located in the former Jewish quarter. The rooms are decorated in a medieval theme. Landlord Biggi has been married to a Rhodian for more than 40 years and is a font of local knowledge. Taxis have access to the hotel.

LÍNDOS & THE SOUTH

BEACHES, TEMPLES & MUCH MORE

In summer, the unbelievably beautiful village of Líndos attracts huge crowds of tourists who make their way either on foot or by donkey up to the world-famous acropolis. In contrast, very few holidaymakers set foot in any of the other mountain villages in the island's south. The modern beachside hotels in Kiotári and Plimmíri are mostly all-inclusive affairs.

From the party vibes on the splendid sandy beach in Líndos and the windsurfers in Prassoníssi at the island's most southerly point to

A view that makes you yearn for the Greek islands: Líndos

the solitary Cape Foúrni and the hippy, laid-back beach bar near Gennádi – Rhodes caters for every taste. The landscape is equally diverse. Monólithos feels like Switzerland by the sea, while the region around Kattaviá resembles the African savannah. Líndos is an archaeological treasure; further south there are only a handful of churches, monasteries and castles to appeal to lovers of history and art. Instead, you can ride on donkeys and horses, spot deer on the roadside and soak up the tranquillity on deserted beaches.

LÍNDOS &
THE SOUTH

Κρητηνία
Kritinia

14 Émbonas

52km, 1 hr 10 mins

Άγιος Ισίδωρος
Aghios Isidoros

13 Siána

3 Laér·

The Old Monólithos ★

Ε Λ Λ Α Δ Α
GREECE

● **Monólithos**
p. 74

Ίστριος
Istrios

12 Cape Foúrni

Προφύλια
Profylia

☂☀

Foúrni Beach

Apolakkiá
p. 74

25km, 30 mins

7 Asklipió

Αρνίθα
Arnitha

Βάτι
Vati

Kiotári

15 Skiádi Monastery

43km, 40 mins

8 Gennádi

16 Mesanagrós

● Mojito Beach Bar ★

9 Lachaniá

17 Kattaviá

10 Plimmíri

Prassoníssi **18**

MARCO POLO HIGHLIGHTS

★ **ACROPOLIS OF LÍNDOS**
The postcard motif of Rhodes – with fabulous views far out to sea ➤ p.62

★ **ST. MARY'S CHURCH**
The church in Líndos tells stories like a picture book ➤ p.64

★ **MOJITO BEACH BAR**
A different kind of all-inclusive place: although you pay, your day at the beach will exceed your wildest expectations ➤ p.72

★ **THE OLD MONÓLITHOS**
First-class taverna in Monólithos, off the beaten track ➤ p.75

LÍNDOS

(🖩 F11) **Líndos (pop. 800) is the most beguilingly beautiful village on the island. Above the village, the acropolis rock is crowned by an elegant temple behind mighty fortifications.**

The whitewashed village sweeps up the green hillside from two beaches below, with the acropolis on one side and the tomb rocks on the other. Nightlife pulses in the narrow lanes long after the village's 80 donkeys have gone home for a well-earned rest.

SIGHTSEEING

ACROPOLIS OF LÍNDOS ★

By donkey or on foot? It's your choice entirely, but ascend you must if you want to see the most spectacular acropolis outside of Athens.

The way up is well signposted and begins right behind the ticket booth. A tiny terrace overlooking the village's golden sands is the perfect spot to catch your breath and take a photo of a relief carved into stone of an ancient war ship. The carving is a tribute by the locals to their Admiral Agesandros who scared off pirates lurking in the waters around Rhodes at the beginning of the second century BCE.

A steep flight of stairs, with medieval history on your right and ancient history on your left, climbs up to the acropolis from the ship's relief. You then reach the entrance gateway of the Knights of St John. The knights had little time for antiquity and believed temples to be pagan in essence, so they basically flattened

Fragments of the temple on the acropolis which have been beautifully restored

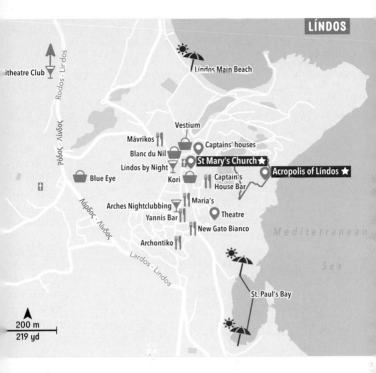

LÍNDOS

Rodos - Lírdos

itheatre Club

Lindos Main Beach

Vestium

Mávrikos
Blanc du Nil
Lindos by Night
Blue Eye
Kori
Captains' houses
St Mary's Church ★
Acropolis of Líndos ★
Captain's House Bar

Arches Nightclubbing
Yannis Bar
Maria's
Theatre
New Gato Bianco
Archontiko

Lardos - Lindos

Mediterranean
Sea

St. Paul's Bay

200 m
219 yd

the ancient relics they found here and built their own fortifications. The Danish, Italians and Greeks restored the site over the last century and reconstructed the columns to give a good impression of what the ancient acropolis once looked like. The information boards which display reconstruction drawings help the imagination. When you walk up the wide flight of stairs to the highest plateau, just imagine living in ancient times and making the pilgrimage to the small temple of Athena Lindia, the town's patron saint. You would only have gained a glimpse of the columns (only some of which have been reconstructed) shortly before reaching the

peak because your view would have been obstructed by a colonnaded walkway or stoa, 87m in length and extending across the entire acropolis. The sight must have been enough to take your breath away.

Relax and take in the view overlooking St Paul's Bay, which was the ancient port of Líndos. In year 51, the apostle Paul landed here when he visited Rhodes. The entire village now stretches out below you, offering the perfect aerial photo opportunity. *April–Oct daily 8am–7.40pm, Nov–March Tue–Sun 8.30am–2.40pm | April–Oct admission 12 euros, Nov–March 6 euros, donkey ride uphill 6 euros, downhill 7 euros | ⊙ 1 hr*

Luxury homes in the lanes of this picturesque village: the Captains' Houses

CAPTAINS' HOUSES

A halfway decent house in Líndos sells for nothing less than one million euros: a fact which has seen the rich and wealthy from all over the world return to the town. These highly priced properties were originally built by Lindian merchants and captains who sailed to all corners of the globe. The carved-relief façades and doors are evidence of their wealth and prosperity. From the inside courtyard, paved with a mosaic of black and white pebbles, you enter the living areas.

The *sála*, the largest room in the house, is always located opposite the entrance. This is where the family slept and where guests were received. The walls of the *sála* were decorated with precious, painted ceramic plates. The oldest were probably brought back by

sailors as souvenirs from Turkey; later, potters from Líndos are said to have produced their own, famous "Lindian plates". They were not meant for eating off, but as wall decorations, so they have a recess in the back on which the plate can be hung by a nail. Modern versions are to be had in every ceramics atelier and souvenir shop.

Some of these old architectural gems are today rented as holiday homes. If you're lucky, you may catch a glimpse inside one when you walk by. The only captain's house open to the public is the café *Captain's House Bar* (see p.65).

ST MARY'S CHURCH ★

As the legend goes, there was once a young devout man who was so attractive that he was persistently chased by the women. However, he wanted to remain celibate so he asked God for his help. In return, God placed a dog's head on the man's head and he was then left alone. This man is known to most as Saint Christopher, the patron saint of travellers. In St Mary's Church in Líndos (15th century),

INSIDER TIP
A holy dog

he is depicted in the bottom row of saints on the right-hand side wall. The other 80 frescoes on the walls and in the dome were painted around 1800 and also tell interesting stories. On the back wall, you can see how the righteous are led by Peter into paradise and how the sinners are transported by fire into the mouth of a monster where hell's punishment awaits them. More cheerful are the illustrations of the biblical story of Creation in the uppermost rows of images. The pictures here tell how God created the world, the animals and the first man, Adam. The pictures would also have you believe that Eve was made from one of Adam's ribs – something you can discuss in your next coffee break. *Daily 9am–5pm | admission free | on the main alley |* ⊙ *15–20 mins*

THEATRE

On the lookout for more traces of ancient history? This open-air theatre with a former seating capacity of 2,000 houses the remains of 27 rows of seats and is evidence of the prosperity of this town 2,300 years ago. It lies at the foot of the acropolis rock and provides the perfect backdrop if you are sitting at one of the cafés on the square. ⊙ *5 mins*

EATING & DRINKING

Beauty has a price. Eating out on rooftop terraces and in the courtyards of captains' houses is a little more expensive than elsewhere on the island – but snacks and gyros are also available here at affordable prices.

ARHONTIKO

No matter whether you order langoustine and succulent steaks or just vegetables and stuffed vine leaves, the proprietor Dímitris and wife Flora treat all their guests the same. The atmosphere is for everyone to enjoy: tables are set on the gallery of a traditional Lindian living area, in the courtyard or on small terraces with a fine view of the illuminated acropolis.

Open daily | main alley Ágios Pávlos 488, upper part | tel. 22 44 03 19 92 | arhontikolindos.com | €€€

CAPTAIN'S HOUSE BAR

Owner Sávvas dreams of one day leaving his business in the hands of his children and spending all his days fishing. His tiny café bar in front of the old captain's house has a laid-back atmosphere where you can sit and relax while pondering on the decorated façades. Don't forget to ask if you can see the *sala* with its splendid wooden ceiling at the other end of the courtyard. Sávvas speaks excellent English and enjoys chatting with his guests when they stop off for a drink on the

> INSIDER TIP
> A beautiful house

The spire of St. Mary's Church is a marker above the rooftops

way down from the acropolis. *Open daily | Odós Akroleos 243 | tel. 22 44 03 12 35 | €€*

MARIA'S

Unpretentious, affordable, well-established taverna in the upper part of the village. There may not be a fine view, but you are more than compensated by the fine Greek food on your plate. *Open daily | Odós Agíou Pávlou | on the alley leading down from Yannis Bar | tel. 22 44 03 13 75 | €€*

MÁVRIKOS

The very first fine-dining taverna to open in Líndos is still the town's most popular address. With views of the beach, acropolis and village, many a celebrity has dined on the restaurant's veranda. The oven-baked lamb as well as all types of fish and seafood are delicious – such as the sea urchin salad or swordfish in caper sauce. *Open daily | on the small roundabout at the village entrance | tel. 22 44 03 12 32 | €€€*

INSIDER TIP
Neither spikes nor bones

NEW GATO BIANCO

Looking for the best Italian on Rhodes? Then go no further than the "new white cat" in Líndos. Finest, authentic Italian cuisine, pizza from the wood-fired oven, all served in a traditional setting on a rooftop terrace overlooking the acropolis. Great hospitality and service. *Daily noon–3pm and from 6pm | on the square in front of the ancient theatre | tel. 69 34 56 22 53 | €€–€€€*

YANNIS BAR

The only bar in town open all year round from morning to well into the night, and a meeting point for locals and tourists alike. Its small terrace is the perfect spot to watch the village's comings and goings. You may see some locals working "out of office" on their laptops. Small snacks are available 24/7. *Open daily | Odós Agíou Pávlou | tel. 22 44 03 12 45 | €€*

SHOPPING

BLANC DU NIL

The white clothing of this international fashion label blends in perfectly in the whitewashed village of Líndos. It could even be used as camouflage. *On the main alley between the donkey "parking lot" and the church*

BLUE EYE

In-vogue Greek fashion designers sell their creations here. Precarious shoes and sandals by Aléxis Tsoúbos, fun summer dresses by Élena Kordáli, extravagant bikinis by Christina Kántova … Come and have fun trying on some new outfits. *On the main alley near the church*

INSIDER TIP
Buy Greek

KORI

This boutique has brought together accessories and souvenirs from Greek artists and designers "to promote the Greek spirit around the world". Take a look inside and decide for yourself if you want to support them in their mission. *Beneath St Mary's church*

Checklist for St.Paul's Bay: sun, beach, sea!

VESTIUM

Casual or business fashion for young women. A mixture of young and established Greek fashion designers share the shelves in this boutique. *Main alley, directly behind the donkey station*

SPORT & ACTIVITIES

LÍNDOS WATERSPORTS

Lovers of water sports staying in Líndos are taken by *Lindos Watersports* to their station 7km away at the Hotel Lindos Princess on Lárdos Beach. They offer jetski and waterskiing, windsurfing, catsailing and fun rides. *Tel. 69 80 08 47 24 | somins-watersports.com*

BEACHES

Both sandy beaches on large Líndos Bay are beautiful, but pretty crowded: ✱ *Líndos Main Beach (also accessible by car)* and the smaller *Pállas Beach (only accessible on foot)*. Both offer water-sports facilities. On the other side of the village, on the heart-shaped ✱ *St Paul's Bay (Ágios Pávlos)*, there are two small pebbly, sandy beaches; day trippers don't come here very often.

WELLNESS

ELXIS SPA

The wonderful wellness centre in the first-class *Hotel Lindos Blu*, including

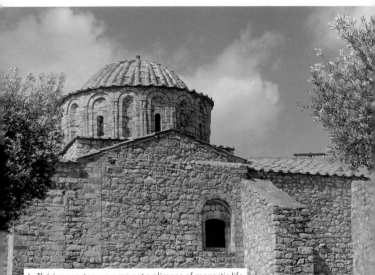
In Thári monastery you can get a glimpse of monastic life

its panorama relax lounge, is open to non-residents. In this spa you don't pay for individual treatments, instead you book package deals for between four and ten hours which allow you to choose your preferred treatments. *Vlícha Beach | tel. 22 44 03 21 10 | lindosblu.gr*

ENTERTAINMENT

AMPHITHEATRE CLUB ⚑
First, it's starry skies, then a laser show, then the sun climbs out of the sea – clubbing à la Líndos. The large open-air club stands high above Líndos Bay with a view of the town and the illuminated acropolis. Good DJs and many live concerts in August. *July/Aug daily midnight–7am | on the road towards Rhodes Town, 2km out of town | amphitheatrelindos.gr*

ARCHES NIGHTCLUBBING
Young islanders come to party under the arches of a traditional Lindian house. The club plays funk, house, hip-hop and R 'n' B. The best parties are held on Saturdays when the local clubbers are **INSIDER TIP** **Saturdays a best** at home. *Daily from 10pm | 10m from the Odós Agíou Pávlou near the Yannis Bar | FB: Arches Plus*

LÍNDOS BY NIGHT
Classic cocktail bar in the middle of the village. Three floors, a rooftop terrace and green lights that make you feel like you're in a rainforest. You can work up a sweat while dancing between the tables. *Daily from 6pm | on the alley that climbs up next to the donkey station | lindosbynight.com*

AROUND LÍNDOS

1 PÉFKI

5km from Líndos / 10 mins by car
Péfki is the perfect beach holiday destination. Indeed, the only attraction is its long sandy beach which is divided into small coves by rocks. There is no old village or any sights; the resort is solely geared to the needs of summer holidaymakers with all the usual water-sport stations along the coast, as well as small hotels, restaurants, cafés and bars along the main road. You can walk to Líndos in 90 minutes or explore the island's south by scooter or car.

The best restaurant to enjoy dinner at is the *Ártemis Garden (daily from 6pm | on the main through road | tel. 22 44 04 83 65 | €€)*, where you can also get excellent pizza. At *Tsambikos (daily from 6pm | below the road to Líndos | tel. 22 44 04 82 40 | €€)* vegetarians will also enjoy themselves; the great food is only topped by a far-reaching view over the town and the sea from the large roof terrace. Later in the evening, *Péfkos by Night (open daily | FB: Pefkosbynight)* is the popular venue in the village centre playing hits from the 1960s to the latest mainstream pop on its veranda. *F11*

2 LÁRDOS

7km from Líndos / 15 mins by car
Although certainly not beautiful, Lárdos has an authentic charm.

Kafenías and tavernas serving rustic food cluster around the village square in the old town on the side of the coastal road that faces away from the sea; there is also life in the village during the winter months. Particularly good, as well as reasonably priced, is the taverna *Savvas (open daily)* where you can get *moussaká* for only 6 euros and a pork chop for 7 euros.

The new Lárdos town is situated 2km away along the beach to Péfki. On the way you pass a small *local heritage museum (daily 9am–3pm | admission 3 euros | ⊙ 15 mins)*, which shows how the inhabitants used to live in Lárdos. *E11*

3 LAÉRMA

22km from Líndos / 30 mins by car
This village lies almost in the centre of the island. There's nothing going on, but it's worth stopping off to visit the taverna *Ingo (open daily | on the main road towards Thári Monastery | tel. 22 44 06 10 71 | €)* for a taste of excellent Rhodian cooking. It was named after a mountain. The landlord, Panayótis and his wife Stamatía will serve you excellent *pitaroúdia*, a kind of spicy veggie burger, or grilled vegetable platter.

INSIDER TIP
Vegetarian specials

Then head along the tarmac road to the nearby ☛ *Thári monastery (daily 8am–sunset | freely accessible | ⊙ 15 mins)* hidden away from sight in the forest. Enjoy the hospitality of the monks and admire the well-preserved frescoes inside the ancient church which dates back to the 14th century.

Return to Láerma and follow the well-signposted path through the forest to the *Elpida Ranch (see p. 33)* a relaxing place surrounded by nature where you can try your hand at horse-riding or archery. The ranch is owned by a friendly couple who warmly welcome you into their home.

4 IPSENÍS

12km from Líndos / 25 mins by car

The small, white nunnery 5km west of Lárdos is not what you'd call a major attraction in itself. It was built in the 19th century and the bell tower was added in the 1960s. What makes it worth a visit, though, is the journey through olive groves and pinewoods. The nuns are hospitable, and the area around the nunnery exudes a sense of peaceful tranquillity. The experience is made more memorable if you climb the gentle slope, following the pilgrims' route past the stations of the cross. *Daily 8am–12.30pm and 4–6.30pm* | ▱ E11

> **INSIDER TIP**
> **Good for the soul**

5 GLÍSTRA BEACH 🌴

12km from Líndos / 15–20 mins by car

This crescent-shaped sandy beach near Kiotári is devoid of hotels, and you can enjoy an unspoilt view of the bay. It has become a popular stop among tourists travelling around the island due to its location directly below the coastal road. It is advisable to follow the crowds. ▱ E11

6 KIOTÁRI

16km from Líndos / 25 mins by car

In summer a 🚂 train passes through Kiotári, which curiously transports more cuddly toys than paying guests. Not content with owning just one attraction in this all-inclusive hotel resort, the train operator has also built the village's only other sight, a large knight's castle *villa (not open to the public)* which stands on the left-hand side of the road when you leave the village in the direction of Asklipió.

Since most of the hotels are all-inclusive, the resort has very few tavernas and bars. If you are not housed in one of these complexes, it' only worth stopping at the shopping centre located next to the sea along the coastal road. There you'll find a silver jewellery workshop *Timo Al*

Frescos illustrate stories from the Bible: St Mary's Church in Asklipió

(Mon–Sat 10am–1pm and from 5pm | timoalb.com); Timo Alb works a lot with operculum, the lid of a species of sea snail. Here you can also have your favourite beach pebble or seashell set in silver for an affordable price. You can watch it being made – a very personal souvenir. *D11*

7 ASKLIPIÓ

21km from Líndos / 30 mins by car

Apocalypse now! The original biblical apocalypse is on display in the 300-year-old *St Mary's Church (15–20 mins)* dedicated to the Feast of the Dormition of the Virgin Mary (Assumption) in Asklipió. A devout man in the 17th century painted the scene inside the church; images include the Riders of the Apocalypse and the Antichrist rising from the depths of the Earth. The other walls of the church also resemble a picture book, adorned with saints and scenes from the Old and New Testament.

Right next to the church there are three small *museums (Mon–Sat 9am–7pm, Sun from 10.30am | admission 1.50 euros | 15 mins)* which are all worth a visit: the Museum of Sacred Art, containing icons and old liturgical books (Evangeliaria), the Museum of Popular Art with an interesting collection of agricultural implements, and an old olive press.

Opposite the church and museums, you can enjoy authentic Rhodes food in the modern taverna *Nikóla (open daily | €)*. Try the sausages served with lemon instead of mustard. After a good meal, you should be ready for the short climb up to the signposted castle ruins, from where you are treated to splendid views of the coast and sea. While you are visiting Asklipió, experience a unique kind of cruise by donkey. *Donkey Cruise* is organised by families

INSIDER TIP
A different kind of cruise

from the region who rescued a group of older donkeys and gave them a new home. The stronger ones are used to carry tourists on excursions lasting one and a half to three hours through the region past old watermills and tiny chapels. Alternatively, you can just visit the donkeys to feed and stroke them. *Donkey Cruise (90-min ride 30 euros, accompanying pers. 10 euros, 3 hrs incl. picnic 40 and 20 euros respectively | 200m off the road from Asklipió to Laérma, signposted from there | appointments: tel. 69 44 86 10 56 or tel. 69 46 43 91 55 | donkeycruise. com | ᗐ D11)*

🖪 GENNÁDI
21km from Líndos / 30 mins by car

A lively village where you can stay in small hotels and holiday homes above the coastal road yet in close proximity to the beach. A traditional place, warts and all, where messy bundles of electrical cables hang from the crumbling façades. Days are spent down on the long pebble-sand beach while the village comes alive in the evenings along its small main street where the sounds from the *Cocoon Lounge & Music Bar* are drowned out by the bass tones from the *Southcoast Music Café* diagonally opposite.

Although you don't have to stop in Gennádi if you're on a tour of the island, one place you must visit is the ★ *Mojito Beach Bar (mid-May-Sept daily round the clock | tel 69 57 67 26 82 | mojitobeachbar.gr | €)* between Gennádi and Lachaniá

If you just want to have a day off and do nothing, the Mojito Beach Bar is the perfect place

A large sign and pink tractor on the coastal road point the way. Aloe vera grows by the house, which proprietor Andréas and his wife Dóra use for their freshly squeezed juices and special mojitos. Brightly coloured tables and chairs stand outside between the veranda and sea on wooden platforms under the trees. Drinks and snacks are also served to the sun loungers. Guests can relax in the hammocks or even stay the night in one of the seven cabanas. Live performances by a Peruvian band are held every week, and some of the regular guests even bring their own instruments with them. If you decide not to leave, you can spend the night in one of the basic rooms. *D12*

9 LACHANIÁ

30km from Líndos / 40 mins by car

Have you ever dined with a priest before? Although the village taverna *Acropole chez Chrissis (open daily | main through road | tel. 22 44 04 60 32 | €)* officially belongs to his wife, the priest often helps out in the restaurant, peeling potatoes, washing vegetables and is always willing to be photographed in his robes. Or you can order just a coffee here and then drive down to his village church where right next door is the modern *Plátanos (open daily | tel. 22 44 04 60 27 | €€)* restaurant serving some of the island's best Rhodian cuisine. *C13*

ER TIP
selfie with
e Reverend

10 PLIMMÍRI

35km from Líndos / 45 mins by car

Up until 2015, Plimmíri was a tiny hamlet, home to a harbour, a handful of fish tavernas and a few houses nestled in the surrounding fields. This all changed however with the opening of an enormous hotel complex called *Tui Magic Life* in the middle of nowhere. The region has attracted no new businesses or tavernas because the entire hotel village is all-inclusive. However, Plimmíri's long pebbly beach can accommodate many sunbathers and the *fish taverna (open daily | €€–€€€)* continues to serve authentic, rustic food. The ruins of a monastery (founded in 1837) stand immediately behind the taverna. Many elements of an early Christian basilica were incorporated into its well preserved *church*, as Plimmíri was a small town 1,500 years ago. Collecting shells is still a popular pastime on the beach and glass bottom boat rides to *Prassoníssi (40 euros | tel. 69 46 25 94 09 | FB: Rhodes Glass Bottom Boat)* are a new attraction. Boats stop off at the desolate *Paradise Beach* and at a wreck of a traditional kaíki boat.

11 VLÍCHA BAY

3km from Líndos / 5 mins by car

Several large hotel complexes are located along the wide 1-km-long pebbly beach at Vlícha Bay. Most of the hotels deceivingly incorporate the word Líndos into their names, yet you can't even see Líndos from this bay – and there is no path leading to the idyllic town 3km away. *F10*

APOLAKKIÁ & MONÓLITHOS

(□ A–B 10–11) **Rhodes can offer refuge away from the masses – the neighbouring mountain villages of Apolakkiá and Monólithos are ideal for this.**

You can stay in small hotels, will quickly get to know the locals and are guaranteed a peaceful night's sleep. Large, by Rhodian standards, the inland village of Apolakkiá (pop. 600), like Monólithos (pop. 330), has only been discovered as a tourist destination in the last few years. Daily life here goes on at a gentle pace as the people make a living largely from the cultivation of cereals, honeydew melons and watermelons.

SIGHTSEEING

CASTLE RUINS

The knights built their castles in some truly amazing locations. In Monólithos they chose a gigantic stone finger which towers over the surrounding barren landscape. Don't worry though; the way up to the castle is harmless, involving a five-minute walk from the road up a rocky path. Only the outer walls, a whitewashed chapel dedicated to St George and a few other ruined buildings have survived.

INSIDER TIP
Stunning sunsets

The best time to enjoy the view across the sea is just before sunset. *Freely accessible during the day | on the road to* Cape Foúrni | Monólithos | ○ 40–55 mins

ÁGIOS GEÓRGIOS VÁRDAS

Do you "collect" churches? This tiny single-nave church in the woods is of art-historical importance. Inside, frescos which date back, like the building itself, to the 13th century remain intact. They depict scenes from the life of Christ and also the Virgin Mary. Other figures include St George, to whom the church is dedicated. *Permanently accessible | 1.3km beyond the Platía of Apolakkiá on the road to Monólitho, signposted from the opposite direction and reached via a 2.7-km-long dirt road | ○ 10–15 mins*

There is not much left of the former castle of the Knights of St John on Mount Monólithos

ÁGIOS GEÓRGIOS KÁLAMOS 🚩

St George's Chapel, entirely decorated with paintings, has no artistic value, but lies in an idyllic spot above the west coast and offers a panoramic view towards the large neighbouring island of Kárpathos – a good place for a picnic. *Freely accessible | 900m off the road between Apolakkiá and Monólithos; well signposted | ⏱ 0–30 mins*

EATING & DRINKING

THE OLD MONÓLITHOS ⭐

The food served here is something special. The proprietors, Manólis and Déspina, lived for a long time in South Africa, and their travels have influenced their cooking. They use only fresh, regional ingredients and all traditional recipes have a refined touch. Their stuffed courgette flowers, which they serve between May and August, are a true delicacy as are, for the more adventurous, the snails which they collect after rainfall. *Open daily | by the village church | Monólithos | tel. 22 46 06 12 76 | €*

BEACHES

You will need a car in order to get to the sea from both villages. The nearest beautiful beaches are at Cape Foúrni.

AROUND APOLAKKIÁ & MONÓLITHOS

12 CAPE FOÚRNI

7km from Monólithos / 15 mins by car

Experience breath-taking scenery on the zig-zag drive down to the Cape. You can clearly mark out the beaches and the Cape from above. A sign on the first of the two beaches, *Alyki Beach*, reads "Please keep it wild", a fitting description also for the beach's tiny bar. Nobody cares how you choose to bathe down here. Just before the road ends at the second beach, the 400m *Foúrni Beach*, you can spot an ancient relief on a rock to the right. It shows the ferryman, Cháron, taking the souls of the dead across the Acheron river to the underworld. What many people don't know: a path (easily walkable with sturdy shoes) criss-crosses the peninsula, leading to antique graves and a cave church. *A10*

INSIDER TIP
Antique graves by the sea

13 SIÁNA

5km from Monólithos / 10 mins by car

Swarms of tourist buses stop-over in Siána on their tour of the island. Reason enough to keep on driving - the village offers no attractions. *B10*

Island life has changed little in the villages between Monólithos and Apolakkiá

14 ÉMBONAS

*21km from Monólithos / 30 mins
by car*

This large village (pop. 1,200) on the western slopes of the Atáviros (the highest peak on Rhodes) was once one of the most original and authentic on the island. Residents made a living from wine growing, animal husbandry and textile weaving. The wine growers and farmers are still here, but the original character of the place has been lost, thanks to the building of numerous (some as yet unfinished) new buildings. Émbonas is no longer a "must-see" destination.

If you do come, however, visit one of the wineries along the main road – although not necessarily the ultra-modern Emery winery, which is popular with bus-tour groups. Wine tasting here takes place against an industrial backdrop; in the smaller establishments, things are far cosier.

You can eat well at the *butcher-cum-taverna (open daily | signposted | tel. 22 46 04 12 47 | €€)* run by the Bákis brothers in the centre of the village. They only use meat from the region, including venison in the winter months. ▢ C8

15 SKIÁDI MONASTERY

*10km from Apolakkiá / 15 mins
by car*

This inland monastery is famous as the place on Earth where the icon of the *Panagía Skiadiní* (Mother of God) is kept – when she is not on tour, as she likes to travel. According to local popular belief, she performs true acts of wonders. The famous icon on the iconostasis cannot be overlooked: gilded and wrought rolled silver entirely cover the figures of the Virgin Mary and the Baby Jesus, except for their face and neck. Many votive offerings are placed near them.

In the weeks leading up to Easter, the Virgin is brought for one or more days to the surrounding villages according to a strictly regulated plan where it stays in the church or the private houses of generously donating locals. This is supposed to give the entire community God's blessing. Ascetic visitors can also spend a night in one of the monastery's basic yet clean cells *(donations welcome)* in the summer. The sunset from here is spectacular and well worth the walk up. *On the tarmac road from the west coast to Mesanagrós | ☉ 20–30 mins | ▢ B12*

INSIDER TIP
A night in the monastery

16 MESANAGRÓS ▶

*14km from Apolakkiá / 20 mins
by car*

The clocks must have stopped here around the end of World War II. The 30 or so inhabitants of the village in the Koukoúliari hills still live in traditional one-room houses. Young people are a rare sight, most of them having moved to Rhodes Town or to one of the holiday idylls on the east coast.

The elderly remain, and are delighted with anyone who has a little time to spare and sits down for a chat at the little coffee house, the *Kafeníon O Tsambíkos (Tue–Sun | €)*.

Prassoníssi in the island's far south is a kitesurfer's paradise

The café owner worked for many years as a hotel bar tender, speaks English proficiently and has many anecdotes up his sleeve to keep guests entertained. He also has the key to open the medieval *church* opposite, which shares many architectural features with early Christian basilicas. An antique column is used as a door lintel, while colourful mosaic remains dating from 500 BCE decorate the courtyard. A small but modern *museum* displays many archaeological artefacts from the region.

Some 3.5km to the south, on the road to Lachaniá, is the tiny *Ágios Thomás* church. His feast day is "Thomas Sunday", the Sunday after Easter, when a popular, bustling parish fair is held under the old cypress trees in front of the church. *B12*

🔟 KATTAVIÁ

17km from Apolakkiá / 15 mins by car

A poor, almost down-trodden village yet with an authentic charm: the *platía* is nothing more than a widening in the road covered in old tarmac. Around the square stand four, usually empty tavernas, the prettiest of which is the *Taverne Penelope (open daily | €)*, resembling a village museum. The best food is cooked by Eftichía and her sons Dimítris and Manólis in *Eftichía (open daily | tel. 69 44 79 43 42 | €)*. The village as well as the plateau on which it stands are North African in influence. The landscape bursts with colour in spring, only to dry out in summer to resemble the African savannah. Head off the main road towards the east coast and you will see the impressive ruins of a large old silk factory standing isolated on your right-hand side. The bell tower of the *Agios Márkos* Church stands on your left towering over the old cowsheds next door

before the war, Kattaviá was the centre of the island's dairy production. *B13*

18 PRASSONÍSSI

25km from Apolakkiá / 20 mins by car
Speed, waves and strong winds – kite- and windsurfers rave about the conditions on this sandy beach, stretching around the island's southern tip. Winds of up to 50kmh are reached in high summer, with waves over 2m high on the eastern side. A paradise for professionals, but beginners should steer well clear. There are three surf centres based in the far south which also organise parties in summer.

Non-surfers can enjoy the view out to sea, hire sun loungers and swim in the designated bathing zone to the east. There are two hostels and three tavernas; wild camping is also tolerated on the beach and sand dunes. Don't worry if you hear some shots ring out – there is a nearby exercise ground or tanks from the Greek army. *B14*

COUNTLESS ACTIVITIES

The place for anyone who wants to be active and sociable: in the evening, the taverna of young land-lord Thomás is the hang-out spot in Monólithos village. Thomás welcomes all of his overnight guests with a glass of Rhodian *soúma* and marinated fruit. He also helps to plan mountain bike tours and hikes, jeep tours and wine tasting. Furthermore, he can get you access to the local telescope where you can track shooting stars with the experts. You'll wish you could extend your stay. *Thomás (Monólithos | in the old village street | tel. 22 46 06 12 91 | thomashotel.gr | 10 rooms | €–€€)*

TREAT YOURSELF!

Experience pure luxury for 250–700 euros per suite between the village and the acropolis of Líndos with a stunning view. This historic house contains many precious items from centuries past, and the garden is just wonderful. When building the house, the owners followed a sustainable approach, using predominantly regional and natural materials. All fabrics in the hotel are made from natural fibres, the bathrooms have organic cosmetics and the waste is separated for recycling. Treat yourself in the *Mélenos Líndos (Odós Akropoléos | tel. 22 44 03 22 22 | melenoslindos.com | 12 rooms | €€€).*

THE CENTRE

THE ISLAND'S QUIETER REGIONS

Rhodes is chameleon in character, changing its appearance constantly as you drive across the island's centre. There are jarring contrasts but also more subtle differences to be seen.

The fertility-bringing, hill-top chapel of Tsambíka and the hotel high-rises in Faliráki stand worlds apart. The eucalyptus avenue that leads into Kolímbia is evidence of meticulous planning, while the maze of old streets in Archángelos suggests a more chaotic side to the island. Unspoilt Tsambíka Beach is almost like a mini Sahara

Holiday soundtrack in Ladikó Cove: waves splashing against the boat

desert by the sea, whereas Profítis Ilías has forested slopes and an Alpine chalet. A visit to the verdant Butterfly Valley can be combined with a short horse ride through a vineyard.

History has left behind a wealth of attractions in this region. Travel back in time on a stroll through the ancient town of Kámiros. Practise your chivalry in one of the castles and be witness to a sad family drama in a tiny Byzantine church. Feeling hungry? Then enjoy fresh fish in Kámiros Skála or the best pizza on the island in Afántou.

THE CENTRE

Mediterranean

Sea

37km, 40 mins

Σορωνή
Soroni

Φάνες
Fanes

Καλαβάρδα
Kalavarda

Kámiros★
p.96

Σάλακος
Salakos

Δίμυ
Dim

Profítis Ilías ★ 12

Άγιος Νικόλαος
Fountoúkli 11

18 Chálki

Μανδρικό
Mandriko

16 Kámiros Skála

17 Kastro Kritínias

Απόλλωνα
Apollona

Κρητηνία
Kritinia

GREE

MARCO POLO HIGHLIGHTS

★ **PETALOÚDES (BUTTERFLY VALLEY)**
At its most beautiful in the butterfly
mating season of July/August, but
always a green oasis ➤ p.88

★ **PROFÍTIS ILÍAS**
Have you come to the wrong place?
Coffee and cakes up in the clouds, with
architecture and forest just like in the
Alps ➤ p.93

★ **KÁMIROS**
A great trio: ancient town, good beach
and tasty food ➤ p.96

Λάερμα
Laerma

Ρόδος
Rhodes

Ιαλυσός
Ialysós

Κρεμαστή
Kremastí

Σγουρού
Sgouroú

Παστίδα
Pastida

Koskinoú **2**

Δαματρία
Damatria

EO95

Μαριτσά
Maritsá

5 Vineyard Triantáfillou

6 Fárma of Rhodes

Καλυθιές
Kalythies

Faliráki
p. 84

Mandomata Beach

4 Petaloúdes (Butterfly Valley) ★

Anthony Quinn Bay **1**

3 Psinthos

Afántou
p. 87

7 Katholikí Afántou

10 Archípolis

άνια
ια

9 Eptá Pigés

Kolímbia
p. 91

30km, 45 mins

Μαλώνας
Malonas

8 Tsambíka

Tsambíka Beach

Archángelos
p. 93

13 Stegná

ΛΑΔΑ

Μάσαρη
Masari

15 Féraklos Fortress

Charáki **14**

EO95

14χμ, 25-30 mins

N

4 km
2.49 mi

In summer, Faliráki is the party capital of Rhodes

FALIRÁKI

(*H6*) **Faliráki is a bustling hive of activity between June and September. The wide, sandy beach stretches for 4km and the island's capital is just ten minutes away by bus – no wonder that the town attracts so many tourists.**

Travel operators have no difficulty finding accommodation for tourists in Faliráki; the town is full to bursting with large hotels. Most of the major multi-storey complexes line the northern end of the beach, while the resort's south is the island's entertainment capital with no end of pubs, sport bars and discos and a few striptease clubs interspersed with stores appropriately named "Alcohol World", as well as pharmacies open 24/7. The tiny harbour in the south hints at the former simplicity of this old fishing village, and is where authentic Greek tavernas can still be found. If you continue along this road, you will come to the island's only official nudist beach and a café for stargazers. The resort offers a diverse mixture of attractions to suit most tastes: you are free to decide what you want to do and what you prefer to avoid.

EATING & DRINKING

AKTÍ 🐷

Mama Paraskeví and her son Nektários remain completely unfazed by the hustle and bustle of the tourist masses. They run their small taverna at the harbour entrance in the traditional Greek manner – with warmth and dedication – and prefer to serve up no-frills, honest-to-goodness fare. Here you are welcome to order just a pint of beer for less than 2 euros. *Open daily | tel. 22 41 08 66 32 | €*

INSIDER TIP **Cheap beer**

STÁMA 🐖

The proprietors of this small taverna have their own fishing boat and offer their catch exclusively here.

INSIDER TIP **Eaten whole**

The sardine-sized *gópes* are usually always on the menu – a delicious freshly fried treat for simple tastes. The fine Greek salad is accompanied by the leaves and twigs of the caper bush – including thorns – marinated in vinegar. Believe it or not, these are not only edible, they are in fact extremely tasty. *Open daily | at the fishing harbour | tel. 22 44 08 64 95 | €€*

STÉFANOS

Among the beach tavernas in front of the gigantic hotels of Faliráki, this one is the best. It is still run by a local family and Élena is in charge of the kitchen. The menu includes a large variety of dishes as well as regional specialities. *Open daily | Odós Apollónos | next to Hotel Apollo Blu | tel. 22 41 08 53 45 | €€*

SHOPPING

There are a host of small supermarkets and souvenir shops, but you should not expect more.

SPORT & ACTIVITIES

All kinds of water sports are offered by the big hotels on the main beach. Speedboats up to 30hp can be hired in the harbour even if you don't have a boating licence.

BEACHES

At more than 4km long and up to 50m wide, Faliráki's main beach extends from the big hotels in the north of the village to the small harbour close to the centre. Either side of this, there are a number of other beaches and rocky coves which you can reach quickly on foot or by bicycle.

If you are not bothered by a rocky coastline with stones beneath your feet when in the water, or if you have packed water shoes, you can walk about 700–1300m from the northern edge of Faliráki, away from the road leading to the thermal spas of Kallithéa, to get to the lovely coves of *Nicólas Beach*, *Tássos Beach*, *Oásis Beach* and *Jordan Beach*. Each beach has a small beach bar and sun loungers along the flat rock plateaus and stony pools. The official ⭐ *Mandomata Nudist Beach* is at the southern end of the bay where umbrellas and sun loungers can be hired.

ENTERTAINMENT

BEDROCK CLUB

Wasn't Bedrock the name of the town where Wilma and Fred Flintstone once lived? Yes, but this club is not your average Stone Age dwelling. Attracting a young crowd of partygoers, the club specialises in themed nights, ranging from beachwear to toga parties. *Open daily | Leofóros Pigón Kallithéas 68*

LIQUID
Clubbers are explicitly invited to dance on top of the bars in this club. Those who prefer to keep their feet firmly on the ground have two dance floors to choose from, playing house and electronic downstairs and R'n'B and hip-hop upstairs. You can chill out on the sofas in the VIP area. *Daily from 11.45pm | Odós Afrodítis 1 | northern street parallel to Bar Street*

MIX CLUB
This club is favoured by holidaymakers from the UK. Laser shows, foam and

paint parties attract revellers, and the sound system is the most powerful on the island. *Open daily from 10pm | Faliraki Shopping Center | Odós Kolokotróni 37*

AROUND FALIRÁKI

1 ANTHONY QUINN BAY
3km from Faliráki / 10 mins by boat
This small, rocky cove near Ladikó got its name because the Greek military junta presented it as a gift to the famous actor – in recognition of the fact that it was here in 1961 that he shot the film *The Guns of Navarone*

The beach at Anthony Quinn Bay has Hollywood appeal

and therefore introduced the island to millions of movie-goers all over the world. The democratically elected government later reclaimed the land, and it is now accessible to all. *On the coastal road in the direction of Líndos, turn left after 1km towards Ladikó; diagonally opposite the Hotel Ladikó, a dirt road leads to the bay | ▥ H7*

2 KOSKINOÚ
7km from Faliráki / 15 mins by car
An authentic Greek village, even this close to Faliráki. The taxi ride to Koskinoú costs just 6 euros and is worth the trip for its maze of narrow lanes with small houses and old mansions. A 20-minute circular walk through the village begins at the church and leads past the local

museum in a typical old residence, as well as the good taverna *O Giánnis (open daily | tel. 22 41 06 35 47 | €).* Head left from the restaurant and then go left again to get back to the village square beneath the church. ▥ H6

AFÁNTOU

(▥ G7) **Afántou is not pretty, yet many of its guests come back year after year.**

They crowd the pavements and the maze of one-way streets, which are virtually devoid of parking spaces, undisturbed by the architectural mayhem surrounding them and the fact that there are no views of the sea from Afántou. They take pleasure in the town's bustling authenticity, know the locals and even have Greek friends. After a day spent on the long stretch of sandy beach, the locals (many of which speak a foreign language) and tourists all come together in the town's many tavernas and coffee houses.

EATING & DRINKING

FOUR SEASONS
This stylishly modern bar serves ample portions of pizza and pasta, and the mixed grill is bombastic. Regular guests order the *kléftiko*, succulent lamb cooked with potatoes and vegetables, which comes fresh from the oven at 6pm every day. *Open daily*

INSIDER TIP
A Rhodian staple

| on the road from the platía to the southern end of the village | tel. 22 41 05 19 90 | €

O THIÓRIS
Looking for a snack to satisfy your hunger? Then head to this traditional white and blue taverna, where the Greek proprietor Theó will inform you what the kitchen has on offer today. Do as the locals do and order a little of everything. Sit in summer under the shady trees, and in winter next to the open fireplace. *Daily from 8pm | Odós El. Venizélou | near the Family supermarket | tel. 22 41 05 33 40 | €*

SERGIO'S
Fancy a pizza? Then try the best on the island here. You can even order takeaway pizza to be delivered to your own apartment. *Daily from 1pm | 20m from the main square | tel. 22 41 05 20 50 | €*

SPORT & ACTIVITIES

In high season, there are a few watersport possibilities. The island's only golf course, the *Afandou Golf Course (April–Oct 35 euros, Nov–March 20 euros | afandougolfcourse.com)* is located between the Rhodes–Líndos road and the beach.

BEACHES

The pebbly *Afántou Beach* is 40m wide and 4km long. It offers no shade at all, but there's still a lot of room since loungers, hotels and tavernas are not yet packed tight. Once an hour in the daytime, 🚃 a miniature train on wheels (ride: 5 euros) plies the route from the village square to the beach.

AROUND AFÁNTOU

3 PSÍNTHOS
8km from Afántou / 40 mins by bicycle
Psínthos is the place to go for a rural dinner. For the Rhodians, the inland village surrounded by green is a historical location. It was here that the Italians defeated the Turks in 1912 and brought the island under their control. It took another 30 years for the island to become Greek.

On the edge of the village, you can dine year-round in pleasant, rustic surroundings at the *Artemída House (open daily | tel. 22 41 05 00 03 | €)* on the road to Archípolis. The regional delicacy of stuffed kid, roasted in the oven for 12 hours, is delicious, as is the roast leg of pork. Salads and vegetables are from the owners' own garden or from friends who farm in the village. *F7*

4 PETALOÚDES (BUTTERFLY VALLEY) ★
16km from Afántou / 25 mins by car
A good choice! Between June and August, hundreds of thousands of butterflies (in Greek *petaloúdes*) populate 5km of this lush, green valley. Usually, they sit with their wings closed, quite inconspicuous, on the

Petaloúdes - speed dating for butterflies

leaves of the sweet gum tree; at other times they fill the air – and sometimes the kitchen of the taverna – in dense swarms! The insect in question is in fact a moth with black front wings and glowing orange back wings, *Panaxia quadripunctaria* – or Jersey Tiger, to give it its English name.

The beautiful countryside is worth a visit at any time of the year. It has a small *Natural History Museum (only May–Oct | visit included in the admission to the valley)* with a butterfly collection and an idyllic taverna *(€)*. The spaghetti served up by proprietor Theófilos, who has run the taverna with his wife and his son Dímitri since 1948, is top class, as is the moussaká, prepared fresh every day.

ȠER TIP
rfect pasta

Mid-June–mid-Sept daily 9am–6pm, otherwise until sunset | admission mid-June–mid-Sept 5 euros, May–mid-June and mid-Sept–Oct 3 euros, Nov–March free admission, but only open sporadically | 🕐 *1–2 hrs |* 📖 *F6*

5 TRIANTÁFYLLOU ☂

19km from Afántou / 30 mins by car

Anastasía Triantáfyllou, daughter of the vinicultural dynasty, Emery, is a passionate wine grower. Her son Jáson even studied viticulture for three years in Bordeaux. Anastasía is almost always to be encountered in this winery established in 1995 on the main road along the west coast to Butterfly Valley; she lets her customers taste the wines, sells homemade wines and the distilled spirit *soúma*,

You get great views from the Tsambíka Chapel on the peak

olive oils and marinated olives as well as a wide selection of natural Greek products including soap made from donkey's milk, mastic gum oil or black volcanic ash. Her son Jáson takes time out of his schedule, inviting guests to join him at the vineyard *(entrance/ driveway is 100m before Fárma of Rhodes)*. The view over the vines stretches to the Profítis Ilías mountain. Visitors are welcome to taste all wines, served with accompanying snacks, while the wine producer talks about his ambitious aims for the vineyard, in French or English. The owners like to take their time to show visitors around the site. *Open during the day | tel. 69 73 42 37 68 | estateanastasia.com | ⊞ F6*

INSIDER TIP
Meet the wine grower

🖸 FÁRMA OF RHODES ⚏

19km from Afántou / 30 mins by car
This private animal park offers an interactive experience: you may stroke and feed most of the animals, and children can ride the ponies. There are dromedaries, llamas, wild boars, deer, sheep, goats and many ostriches. The park's taverna serves ostrich omelettes and meat; the shop sells colourfully painted ostrich eggs, as well as creams and oils made from ostrich fat. *Daily 9am–7pm | admission: adults 7 euros, children (age 3–12) 4 euros | well sign-posted on the west coast road to the butterfly valley | farma-rhodes.com | ⏱ 1–1.5 hrs | ⊞ E6*

🖸 KATHOLIKÍ AFÁNTOU

2km from Afántou / 30 mins on foot
Building work on the small church

continued on and off for many centuries. It is worth a visit, above all for the frescos – even if art historians do not consider them to be particularly special. To reach the church, you have to drive past the village, coming from the direction of Rhodes Town. Shortly after the signpost which reads "Afántou Golf" there is a sign for Afántou Beach – turn off here. The church is situated on the left. ⏱ *10–15 mins* | 🗺 *G7*

KOLÍMBIA

(🗺 *G8*) **A 2-km-long road lined with eucalyptus trees leads you into the town of Kolímbia. With over 40 hotels – most of which are all-inclusive – the resort competes with Faliráki and Ixiá yet it has its own distinctive charm.**

Most of the hotels are pleasantly spacious, low-rise complexes set a good distance apart. The town only has a few (yet long) streets, all named after European capitals, and you will find no loud clubs or bars anywhere. The beach is not one long stretch of sand; it divides into two intimate coves.

EATING & DRINKING

TO NISÁKI
The name translates as "small island" and this taverna is dedicated to fish through and through. Most of what the proprietor puts on the tables comes from the Aegean. Next door, he

also runs a bar, and the whole set-up is just a few steps from the beach. *Open daily | at the northern edge of town | tel. 22 41 05 63 60 | €€€*

SPORT & ACTIVITIES

On the main beach north of the village centre *Kolymbia Watersports (tel. 69 37 11 16 41 | kolymbiawatersports. com)* has jetskis and speedboats which you can rent without a boating licence. In this way you can explore the many beaches along the east coast between Faliráki and Líndos.

BEACHES

The beach, which is windy here, is not one long stretch of sand, but it is divided into two sections and has a much more intimate feel than at Faliráki, for example.

AROUND KOLÍMBIA

🖪 TSAMBÍKA 🐾
5km from Kolímbia / 15 mins by car plus a further 10 mins on foot
If you meet somewhere in the world a man named Tsambíko or a woman named Tsambíka, you will know where they come from: Rhodes. And you will also know who was responsible for their conception. The tiny white-washed monastery church on the mountain peak *(⏱ 1-hr return trip)* is a place of pilgrimage to this day and is

visited in particular by young women in the hope of children. While most tourists drive up half the way, female pilgrims walk (or crawl) up to pray for fertility and the chance of a child. It is said that the pilgrimage will be most fruitful if the pilgrim shoulders a sack containing a heavy stone.

A path leads through a white gateway into the monastery courtyard. Women enter their name and their wish in the thick guestbook lying open in the chamber on the right. On the left-hand side there is an empty chamber which serves pilgrims as a dormitory. Tsambíka's miracle-working

If you are longing for a cool place, visit Eptá Pigés

icon of the Virgin Mary is only visible in the church on 7 and 8 November. For security reasons, she stands for the rest of the year in the modern monastery *Káto Tsambíka*, located on the main road to Líndos, just 1km away from the road up to the hilltop chapel.

Between the old and the new monastery, a lane branches off to the unspoilt 🌴 Tsambíka Beach. The sand is so fine that storms have heaved it against a slope at the southern edge of the bay where it resembles a high dune in a desert. The tourist facilities, on the other hand, are anything but barren: improvised beach bars, sun loungers and a water-sports station provide entertainment for all ages. *Ш G8*

9 EPTÁ PIGÉS 👯

6km from Kolímbia / 15 mins by car

It is always pleasantly cool under the huge sycamore trees in the valley of Eptá Pigés ("Seven Springs"). The many peacocks seem to like the environment, too. The feature which attracts visitors to this popular destination is a 186-m-long underground water channel dug during the Italian occupation of the island. At the end of the tunnel is a pond amid a gently rolling, lush green landscape. Walk over the hill above the tunnel to get to this idyllic spot. A word of warning: since the whole area is a protected source of drinking water, you will have to do without taking a dip in the pond.

Directly behind the car park, you'll find the taverna *Seven Springs (open daily | tel. 22 41 05 62 59 | €)*, where you can order simple Greek dishes such as *souvláki* (meat grilled on a skewer) or *paidákia* (lamb chops). *G8*

10 ARCHÍPOLIS 🎪

10km from Kolímbia / 20 mins by car
A different kind of treehouse: In the ancient *sycamore tree* in front of the stairs to the *Ágios Nektários* monastery near the inland village Archípolos, an entire family can fit inside its completely hollowed-out trunk. *F8*

11 AGIOS NIKÓLAOS FOUNTOÚKLI

16km from Kolímbia / 25 mins by car
No house to be seen far and wide, just low-lying rocks and green countryside, but a 600-year-old church stands on the roadside where goats and sheep sometimes congregate in front of the fountain and fruit producers sell their goods: a splendid spot for a small picnic.

Founded by a high-ranking Byzantine official, the church was also the setting for a family tragedy. The official and his wife are depicted on a fresco next to the west entrance. On the opposite wall, the couple's three children are represented. An inscription relates that they all died at around the same time, probably as a result of some kind of epidemic. ⏱ *15–20 mins* | *E7–8*

12 PROFÍTIS ILÍAS ⭐

20km from Kolímbia / 35 mins by car
Are temperatures getting too hot? Then ride up to the island's third highest mountain. At a height of almost 800m, it is pleasant up here even in summer; islanders come to the forest with their children mainly at the weekends. The Italians built a hotel up here in 1929 in the style of an Alpine chalet. Its café serves delicious cakes and desserts. In order to work off those calories, you can take off on a tour of the surrounding forests with the free mountain bikes available to guests. The hotel is called 🛏 *Élafos (tel. 22 41 04 48 08 | elafoshotel.gr | €€).* | *D8*

ARCHÁNGELOS

(*F–G 8–9*) **Archángelos (pop. 5,500) is a good example of how tourism does not have to be synonymous with the disappearance of everything that is fundamental to the charm of a place.**

It shares this aspect with Afántou, yet the historic centre of Archángelos is far more appealing. There are old, whitewashed houses and unevenly paved alleyways. The locals always seem to have time to spare. Old traditions still mean something in the "village of the Archangel" – especially on Good Friday and Saturday as well as on Carnival Sunday. The next beach is 3km away, below the town at Stegná.

SIGHTSEEING

CHURCH

Like a bejewelled, snow-white finger, the bell tower of the church of the Archangel Michael dominates the similarly white houses of the old part of Archángelos. The structure, with its delicate air, is a remnant of the Italian occupation. The church itself dates back to the mid-19th century. The most interesting feature is the typically Rhodian mosaic in the inner courtyard made of black and white pebbles. ⊙ *10–15 mins*

KNIGHTS' FORTRESS 🐾

On a hill on the edge of the village stand the ruins of a castle built by the Knights of St John, commissioned by Grand Master Orsini in the middle of the 15th century. Close to the entrance, several coats of arms are to be seen carved into the walls, including the Orsini crest and the number 1467, the year the castle was completed. From the castle, you have a fine view over the white silhouette of the historical part of the village. It is well suited to a picnic. ⊙ *15–30 mins*

EATING & DRINKING

AFÉNTIKA

This small, unspectacular taverna, in which elderly local residents often get together in the evenings to watch television, serves up a particularly good Greek salad. Made according to the traditional recipe, twigs and leaves from the caper bush, marinated in vinegar, are also added. The proprietor is extremely friendly and often lets you have an ouzo or *soúma* on the house – and consequently has built up quite a following among Archángelos' holiday guests! Dishes that are not actually on the menu can

INSIDER TIP
Deliciously soft thorns

be prepared specially, if ordered in advance. *Open daily | in the centre, tucked away behind the Legend Bar on the road to the Post Office | tel. 22 44 02 36 40 | €*

HELLAS

The owner Stélios grew up in Germany, so his restaurant has some German touches, despite its very Greek name. He makes special dishes for his regulars, and his daughter Stamatía loves the meatballs filled with feta cheese the best. *Open daily | on the side of the town hall | tel. 22 44 02 27 06 | €*

SHOPPING

Traditionally, Archángelos is seen as the island's pottery village. There are a number of ceramics workshops on the main road between Rhodes Town and Líndos.

SPORT & ACTIVITIES

JUNGLE TOUR

Although the jungle tour with Níkos Pápas covers a mere distance of 4km it is packed with unusual experiences After a cup of coffee, Níkos starts the day off with a dancing lesson. Then the actual tour begins, which leads you mostly through a dry riverbed Here, Níkos explains the flora and geology of the location, turning out to be a great, multilingual talker. There are stalls provided by the wayside where you can sustain yourself with fresh fruit. At the end, and following a

INSIDER TIP
An eccentr experienc

Charáki offers sympathetically designed B&Bs below towering castle ruins

cooking lesson, Níkos serves food on tables in the riverbed. *Tour 28 euros incl. food | tel. 69 38 19 00 41 | nikos-papas.nl*

AROUND ARCHÁNGELOS

🖪 STEGNÁ ✱☀

3km from Archángelos / 10 mins by car

This remote beach village can be reached via a winding road. The 500-m-long, sandy beach at Stegná is perhaps not as beautiful as the one at Tsambíka, but the bay is greener and the food at the shady tavernas is down-to-earth, good-quality Greek fare. In the seafood taverna *En Plo (open*

daily | tel. 22 44 02 25 37 | €€) on the coastal road you can order *Germaní*, these brown rabbitfish got their name during World War II thanks to their spikes and camouflage colour. *⊞ G9*

🖂 CHARÁKI

9km from Archángelos / 15 mins by car

Until a few years ago, only a handful of summer houses stood on the pebble beach here. Many of them belonged to farmers from the villages of Malónas and Mássari further inland where people still live from the cultivation of oranges and mandarins. Meanwhile, Charáki has become a popular bathing resort, but without the huge hotel blocks. Visitors stay mostly in small guesthouses and holiday apartments. A pedestrianised beach promenade, with cafés, restaurants and bars, adds to the flair of the village. Take a look at the small *Ágii Apóstoli Chapel* on the village square which was decorated inside in 1997 and 1998 in the traditional style by the monks of the autonomous republic of Mount Athos. *F9*

15 FÉRAKLOS FORTRESS
9km from Archángelos / 15 mins by car

On a hill to the north of Charáki lie the ruins of the fortress of the Knights of St John, Féraklos, which is illuminated in the evening. It is assumed that a castle stood here in the days of antiquity. What is certain is that there was a Byzantine fortress on the site which was captured by the Knights of St John in 1306. In 1470, Grand Master Orsini had it renovated. The fortress was used mostly as a prison for the prisoners of war taken by the Order, and as a place of exile for knights who were guilty of misconduct.

From the north side, there is a beautiful view across the fertile land around Malónas and Mássari and over the bay and sandy beach at the base of the hill. Above the bay, a touching gem is to be found hewn into the rock face: the tiny chapel *Ágia Agáthi* (⏱ *5 mins*). It is said to have been constructed in the 12th or 13th century.

Agáthi Bay, which is a 30-minute walk from Charáki, boasts a pretty, sandy beach. Its 200 metres are usually rather quiet, though three beach bars have set out their tables in the sand. The fortress is most easily reached from the beach access road, but sturdy shoes are recommended. *F9*

KÁMIROS

(*D2*) **Sunbathing and sightseeing – you can get the best of both worlds in ★ Kámiros.**

First visit the excavations in the ancient town, followed by the beach and the waterfront tavernas. You can spend a whole day in the town, which is easily reached by bus.

SIGHTSEEING

EXCAVATIONS

Fed up of temples and ancient Gods? Here you can find out how normal folk lived over two millennia ago. Kámiros was the smallest of the first three Rhodian cities and had its heyday in the 6th century BCE. The town was built on a slope, and the view from the houses spans green fields, pinewoods and olive groves. Inhabitants of the upper part of town could even see the coast. You can still enjoy the same view today because no hotel or industrial plant stands in the way at the moment. The residents, however, paid dearly for their town's exquisitely beautiful location. In 226 BCE, an earthquake destroyed almost every building, but the town was re-built. Around three centuries later, in 142 CE, another major quake razed Kámiros to the ground. This time no one wanted to stay, and Kámiros was abandoned.

The ruins of "Rhodian Pompei" date largely from the 3rd and 2nd century BCE. The lower terrace of this hillside site was hewn into the rock supported by mounds of earth and retaining wall and enlarged to form the agorá, or market place. To each side, there once stood shrines, statues and residential buildings. The small temple in the centre was probably dedicated to Apollo.

To the east of this, there is a festival ground with low tiers of seats for spectators. This was probably the venue for rituals in honour of Apollo. To the west, the arena borders a residential area which lies directly on the ancient main thoroughfare. This leads past a public baths and a fountain house (in many places, ceramic pipes hark back to the ancient water supply and drainage system) and further residential areas as far as the acropolis. Only a few traces of its once magnificent buildings remain. *Approx. Easter–Oct daily*

8am–7.45pm, Nov–Easter Tue–Sun 8.30am–2.40pm | admission 6 euros, Nov–Easter 4 euros | ⏱ 45–70 mins

EATING & DRINKING

OLD KÁMIROS

Located opposite the side road leading to the excavations and directly in front of the bus stop, the more traditional of the two beach-front tavernas is simply furnished yet boasts an extremely friendly service. Langoustines and other shellfish are kept in the large basin. You may be able to negotiate the price with owner Jórgos, as long as you

INSIDER TIP
Open to negotiation

do it away from the other guests. *Open daily | tel. 69 45 41 17 30 | €€*

The inhabitants of ancient Kámiros would have enjoyed the same marvellous views

BEACHES

The beach in front of both tavernas is the nicest food to customers on the free beach sun loungers.

AROUND KÁMIROS

16 KÁMIROS SKÁLA
13km from Kámiros / 15 mins by car
A few isolated houses, an occasional passenger ferry and a handful of fishing boats at the quay in front of the low-lying rocks. The boats sail over from the small islands off the coast of Rhodes, bringing their catches ashore. Refrigerated trucks then transport the fish to the island's hotels and tavernas.

Locals gather on the large veranda of the taverna *Altheméni (open daily | tel. 22 46 03 13 03 | €–€€)*, to eat fish and succulent pork chops served with Greek salad and marinated capers With plenty of room between the tables and Greek music playing in the background, the taverna has hardly changed since 1957 when the

A Mediterranean dream: the village of Nimborió on the island of Chálki

randfather fed the entire family with he catch from his tiny fishing boat which still stands prettily decorated on he veranda. *B8*

⑦ KASTRO KRITÍNIAS 🐷

6km from Kámiros / 25 mins by car
)ating back to the time of the Crusaders, this small castle holds a olitary position overlooking the vast egean Sea. The castle is open to the ublic and is just a two-minute walk rom the car park. You can also spend a eisurely hour on the small shady eranda of the no-name *taverna (€)* eneath the car park. The owner only

serves homemade, traditional Greek food. *Kritinía | ⏱ 20–35 mins | B–C8*

⑱ CHÁLKI

Regular boat service 45–75 mins (depending on the vessel), catamaran 75 mins, 12 nautical miles from Kámiros Skála, 35 nautical miles from Rhodes Town

The tiny island of Chálki is worth the short boat ride. Only 200 people now live there, but the main village of Nimborió is really picturesque. As you enter the harbour, notice the old houses painted in pastel colours. More and more of them are gradually being renovated and rented out as holiday homes.

The local minibus or the island's taxi will shuttle you to the three beaches, to the deserted village of *Chorió* with its Crusaders' castle, and to the monastery *Ágios Ioánnis* in the island's far west. This region shows how rugged and barren the landscape can be on the Greek Aegean islands.

The fastest and easiest way to get to Chálki is to take the *catamaran (12ne.gr)*, which runs several times a week from Rhodes Town. You can also book day-long tours. In summer, a regular daily boat service to the island departs from Kámiros Skála at 9.45am and returns around 4.30pm. *A–B 1–2*

DISCOVERY TOURS

Want to get under the skin of the region? These discovery tours provide a perfect guide – they include great tips for breath-taking sights, stops worth making for the perfect holiday snap, the best places for a bite to eat and fun activities.

❶ RHODES AT A GLANCE

- ➤ A tour round the entire island
- ➤ Say "hello" to antiquity
- ➤ Watch the surfers and go swimming

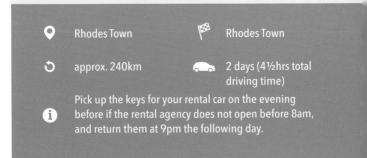

📍	Rhodes Town	🏁	Rhodes Town
🔄	approx. 240km	🚗	2 days (4½hrs total driving time)

ℹ️ Pick up the keys for your rental car on the evening before if the rental agency does not open before 8am, and return them at 9pm the following day.

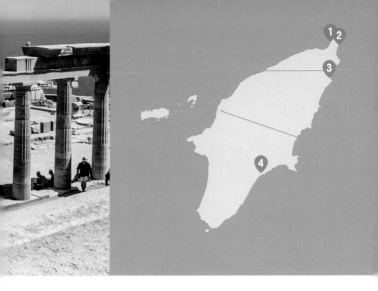

It's not only Athens that has an ancient acropolis. Don't miss Líndos!

START EARLY WHEN IT'S STILL COOL

Depart from ❶ Rhodes Town ➤ p. 38 *in the morning around 8am and head towards the airport. From the centre of Ialissós (Triánda)* ➤ p. 55, *follow the signs up to* ❷ Filérimos ➤ p. 55. The open view of the coast and the island's mountains to the southwest gives you a real feel for the beauty of the Rhodian landscape and offers great photo opportunities.

Head back to the coastal road and follow it until you reach the excavations of the ancient city of ❸ Kámiros ➤ p. 96. It's best to arrive in the early morning because the archaeological site doesn't have any shade. A good place to take a break afterwards is the fishing harbour ❹ Kámiros Skála ➤ p. 98, an ideal spot to watch the local fishermen at work.

UP INTO THE MOUNTAINS & TO THE CASTLE

Afterwards, travel up to the large mountain village of ❺ Siána ➤ p. 76. It is worth taking a short break to admire the church gate which is often covered in a wealth of blossom. *You can park in the car park below the road directly by the church.* Drive on a bit further and climb up to the castle ruins of ❻ Monólithos

❶ **Rhodes Town**
13km 15mins

❷ **Filérimos**
31km 30mins

❸ **Kámiros**
13km 15mins

❹ **Kámiros Skála**
22km 20mins

❺ **Siána**
5km 5mins

❻ **Monólithos**
32 km 40 Min.

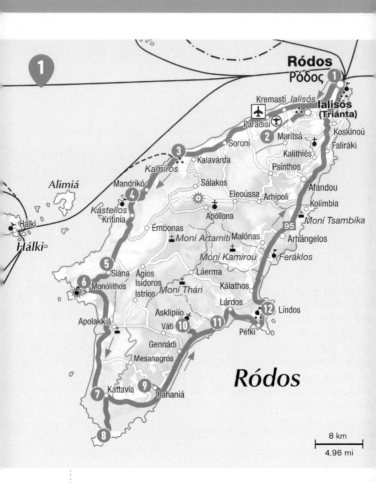

➤ p. 74, from where you can look out over the sea to the neighbouring island of Kárpathos. If all of this has made you hungry, Monólithos is a good place to have some lunch.

DRIVE ON FOR COFFEE IN THE SOUTH

Continue along the open and largely untouched beaches where the winds are sometimes quite strong *to the southernmost point on the island* near **7** Kattaviá ➤ p. 78. After a coffee break on the village square, drive over *the well-paved road through the iso-lated countryside to the island's southern cape* where

7 Kattaviá
9km 15mins

you will find the surfers' beach ❽ Prassoníssi ➤ p. 79, which resembles the Sahara in miniature.

First head back to Kattaviá and, from there, continue on towards ❾ Lachaniá ➤ p. 73. For an authentic culinary experience with a rustic feel, stop in at the taverna Plátanos.

SACRED ART & AEGEAN WAVES
Follow further along the coast towards Kiotári ➤ p. 70, where a small cul-de-sac leads up to ❿ Asklipió ➤ p. 71 The frescos on the walls of the church in this small mountain village are some of the island's most beautiful. *Almost right next door on the coastal road* ⓫ Glístra Beach ➤ p. 70 , one of the prettiest on the Island, will lure you into the water for a swim.

IMMERSE YOURSELF IN PICTURESQUE VIEWS
Shortly before Lárdos ➤ p. 69, turn to the right to head towards Péfki ➤ p. 69 and keep driving through this coastal town to get to ⓬ Líndos ➤ p. 62. As you approach this picturesque village from above, you will see its old captains' houses and countless souvenir shops, as well as St Paul's Bay and the broad main beach below. The ancient acropolis lies before you at about eye-level. You'll now realise why it is worth spending another entire day here.

VISIT A TYPICAL TAVERNA
The road between Líndos and the island's capital makes for an easy and quick drive back to ❶ Rhodes Town where you will arrive around 9pm if you choose to return on the same day. If you do not have to turn in your rental car until the next morning, you should definitely drive on to the large village of Archángelos ➤ p. 93, where you can dine among the locals in one of the country-style tavernas in the centre of town before making your way back to Rhodes Town.

❽ **Prassoníssi**
23km 30mins

❾ **Lachaniá**
18km 15mins

❿ **Asklipió**
9km 10mins

⓫ **Glistra Beach**
➤ **12km** 15mins

⓬ **Líndos**
51km 55mins

❶ **Rhodes Town**

❷ THE OLD TOWN IN DEPTH – A DAY IN THE CAPITAL

➤ Experience the Rhodes of the knights
➤ Explore 5,000 years of history in exciting museums
➤ Relax in beautiful cafés and soak up the atmosphere

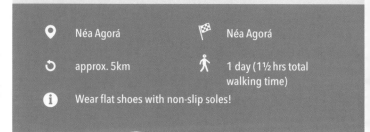

📍 Néa Agorá	🏁 Néa Agorá
↻ approx. 5km	🚶 1 day (1½ hrs total walking time)
ℹ Wear flat shoes with non-slip soles!	

TAKE IN THE VIEW

❶ Néa Agorá

700m

All bus routes from the holiday resorts into town end at the ❶ Néa Agorá ➤ p. 47. First off, *stroll through the inner courtyard* with its many barbecue stands and a handful of jewellers and souvenir shops and make your way to the two kiosks opposite, which boast the largest selection of international newspapers and magazines on the island. *Pass between the kiosks to come out on the harbour side of the Néa Agorá*, which is home to some tempting pastry shops. If you can resist the delicious cakes and ice cream sundaes on offer, *cross the street* and sit down on one of the many benches to take in the colourful array of excursion boats and sailing yachts before you.

❷ Ágios Nikólaos

600m

Then *wander past the restored windmills on the eastern pier to the medieval fortress tower* ❷ Ágios Nikólaos. This is the best place to take a photo of the Old Town centre across Mandráki Harbour ➤ p. 46. You can also get a good snapshot of most of the huge cruise ships docked in the neighbouring Emborikó harbour. That might work well for a selfie.

INSIDER TIP
The big bo

INTERESTING MUSEUMS

Once you are back at the mill pier, *follow the traffic over the short bridge into the Old Town.* Behind the parked cars, it is easy to overlook the remains of an ancient ❸ Aphrodite Temple. Art lovers should head to the right and explore the art gallery of the ❹ Museum of Modern Greek Art ➤ p. 48. Go a few steps further and you will find yourself on the *Platía Argirokástrou.* Alongside the small pyramids of stone cannonballs, this square is home to the first hospital of the Order of the Knights. *Walk straight on for another 50m until you reach the* ❺ Museum of Archaeology ➤ p. 42, which

❸ Aphrodite Temple
40m

❹ Museum of Modern Greek Art
150m

❺ Museum of Archaeology
350m

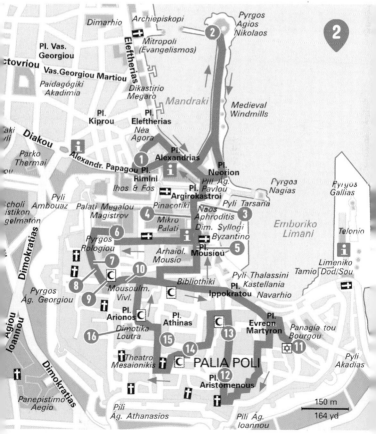

Minaret of the Mosque of Suleiman

was the second, much larger hospital run by the Knights of St John. Even if you are not really into art, you should still definitely take a look. The two-storey arcades of the inner courtyard provide a great photo opportunity, and the large hospital ward of the Order of St John is like no other in the world. A shady garden invites you to have a rest among the greenery.

GIVE YOUR FEET A BREAK & GAIN AN OVERVIEW

The cobblestoned Avenue of the Knights ➤ p. 44 *climbs gently uphill, past the 600-year-old inns of the crusaders to the magnificent* ❻ Palace of the Grand Master ➤ p. 44. *After inspecting the palace, it is time to treat your feet to something special. Head right out of the Palace of the Great Master and go left on Odós Orféos.* Give your feet a break in ❼ Magía Fish Spa ➤ p. 53, courtesy of the small fish in the glass tubs who like to nibble away at your toes. After that, head up to the top of the ❽ Clock Tower ➤ p. 45 to get a good overview of the entire town. The entrance fee includes a refreshing drink.

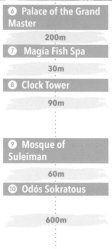

❻ **Palace of the Grand Master**

200m

❼ **Magía Fish Spa**

30m

❽ **Clock Tower**

90m

❾ **Mosque of Suleiman**

60m

❿ **Odós Sokratous**

600m

BROWSING & SHOPPING

The ❾ Mosque of Suleiman ➤ p. 45 with its towering minaret marks the beginning of the most dangerous part of the tour, at least for your bank account. *Head down* ❿ Odós Sokratous ➤ p. 45, where you can shop at your leisure and then shop some more. Shops selling jewellery, leather goods and souvenirs line Socrates Street on both sides. The best places to stop for a snack are the secluded garden café Socratous Garden ➤ p. 50 at the top end of the street, or Café Kárpathos in the middle, where you can sit under shady trees and watch as people from around the world pass by. If you like quaint places, *head down*

Odós Sokratoús for another 20m and check out (on the left) the town's oldest café: Kafenío Bekir Karakusu.

INTO THE JEWISH QUARTER

Socrates Street ends at *Platía Ippókratou* with its expensive cafés. If you order a large beer here, you will be presented with a 4-pint boot-shaped glass. Go past the many souvenir shops along the street until you come to *Platía Evréon Márytron*, with its noisy parrots, in the former Jewish Quarter of the Old Town. *Odós Dossiádou* is home to the fully restored ⑪ Kahal Shalom Synagogue ➤ p. 46. From here, the route *continues through the narrow and winding streets of the town centre*. The rump of an old ⑫ Windmill on *Odós Pythágora* offers a great vantage point from which to gaze over the rooftops of the Old Town and cast your eyes across the sea towards Asia Minor.

FROM THE PASHAS TO AN UNUSUAL LOST-PROPERTY OFFICE

At the end of Odós Pythágora, in the area around the ⑬ Ibrahim Pasha Mosque *(visitors always welcome except during Friday prayers),* you will find the hippest quarter of the Old Town. It might be a little sleepy in the afternoon, but in the evening, it really comes to life. *Follow Odós Sofokléous to get to the* ⑭ Platía Doriéos ➤ p. 46 where the attractive Rejab Pasha Mosque and two pleasant cafés await. *Continue along to the Byzantine church of* ⑮ Ágios Fanoúrios ➤ p. 46. In a way, this church is the town's lost-property office because, on request, Saint Fanoúrios helps people to find lost and forgotten items. After taking a look inside, head past the *Sultan Mustafa Mosque to what were once the* ⑯ Turkish Baths.

Afterwards, you can take another stroll *through the area around Socrates Street*. Spend the rest of the evening in one of the characteristic and enjoyable Old Town tavernas before returning to ① Néa Agorá to catch a bus or taxi back to your hotel.

⑪ **Kahal Shalom Synagogue**

500m

⑫ **Windmill**

250m

⑬ **Ibrahim Pasha Mosque**

250m

⑭ **Platía Doriéos**

200m

⑮ **Ágios Fanoúrios**

150m

⑯ **Turkish Baths**

950m

① **Néa Agorá**

❸ UP & DOWN THE MOUNTAINS

➤ Discover Rhodes as a green island
➤ Enjoy the excellent Rhodian cuisine in a rural taverna
➤ Explore the island's heights by bicycle or on foot

📍 Faliráki   🏁 Faliráki

🔄 c. 110km   🚗 1 day (4 hrs total driving time)

ℹ️ Take a torch and a towel for going through the tunnels, and provisions for a picnic.
Please note that many of the butterflies in Petaloúdes can only be seen from June to August.

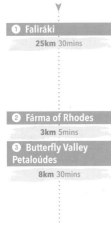

❶ Faliráki

25km 30mins

❷ Fárma of Rhodes

3km 5mins

❸ Butterfly Valley Petaloúdes

8km 30mins

❹ Psínthos

13km 15mins

OSTRICHES & BUTTERFLIES

From ❶ Faliráki ➤ p. 84 , *drive towards the airport. Just past the eastern end of the airport village of Parádissi,* signs clearly point the way to a side road that branches off from the main road and leads towards the Butterfly Valley in Petaloúdes. Especially if you have kids on board, you should take a short detour to see the ostriches and other animals at the ❷ Fárma of Rhodes ➤ p. 90 that lies along the way. Park your car at the lower (first) entrance to ❸ Petaloúdes (Butterfly Valley) ➤ p. 88 and *walk upstream and back down again*. If you take a break for a cup of coffee in the taverna at the lower entrance to the valley, in summer you will probably find yourself surrounded by colourful fluttering wings.

TIME FOR A LUNCH BREAK

Afterwards, drive on the ascending road past the middle and upper entrances to the Butterfly Valley and the abandoned Kalópetras monastery. *As the road contin ues on, it climbs to the top of a pass and then back down to the large village of* ❹ Psínthos ➤ p. 88, *where you can eat lunch on the Platía or in the Artemída House which lies on the road leading to Archípolis.*

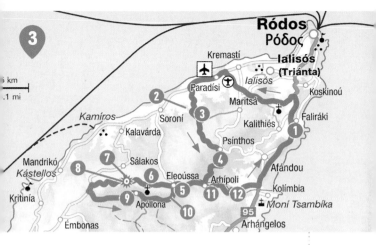

When this side road meets the main road from Kolímbia to Eleoússa, turn right and pass through Archípolis and **❺ Eleoússa** with its abundance of water and Italian-style colonial houses to the isolated Byzantine church of **❻ Ágios Nikólaos Fountoúkli ➤ p.93**, situated between fields and uncultivated land, where you can enjoy a picnic.

CIRCLE THE MOUNTAIN – FOR THE SPORTY

You can enjoy some refreshments at the café of the alpine-style hotel **❼ Élafos ➤ p.93** located in the forests right below the 780-m-high **❽ Profítis Ilías ➤ p.93**. Reinvigorated, you can then circle Profítis Ilías on a narrow tarmac forest road (8.5km long); just follow the signposts to the "Athletic Centre". If the hotel reception

agrees, you can also do it on one of the hotel's rental bikes. Whether by car, bike or on foot: you will experience a mostly unknown part of Rhodes!

OLD VILLAGES & AN EVEN OLDER TREE

After you've returned to the Hotel Élafos, drive to the peaceful mountain villages of **❾ Apóllona** and **❿ Plataniá**. You will then find yourself back in Eléoussa before you again pass through **⓫ Archípolis ➤ p.93**.

❺ Eleoússa	
3km 5mins	
❻ Ágios Nikólaos Fountoúkli	
6km 10mins	
❼ Élafos	
1km 30mins	
❽ Profítis Ilías	
15km 35mins	
❾ Apóllona	
6km 10 mins	
❿ Plataniá	
6km 10mins	
⓫ Archípolis	
6km 10 mins	

Just after you leave the village, look to the right and you will see a hollowed-out  plane tree below the large pilgrimage church of Ágios Nektários, with its decorative frescos. Your children may want to play in the "tree house" and the kiosk nearby sells hot and cold drinks.

INSIDE THE GREEN TUNNEL

Drive through the valley of the streambed of Loutan towards the coast, and then follow the signs to turn towards the forest taverna at ⑫ Eptá Pigés ➤ p. 92. Ducks and peacocks will come out to greet you before you explore the dark tunnel for a bit of an adventure.

⑫ **Eptá Pigés**
14km 20mins

❶ **Faliráki**

At Kolímbia, get back on the eastern coastal road and it is just another 10km back to ❶ Faliráki.

In Ágios Nektários Church you won't know what to look at first

④ CYCLING THROUGH QUIET VILLAGES

➤ Discover rural Rhodes by mountain bike
➤ Admire beautiful small churches and meet the priest
➤ Get to know villagers who are still delighted to encounter holidaymakers

📍 Kiotári   🏁 Kiotári

🔄 55km   🚲 1 day (4½–7 hrs cycling time)

📊 difficult   ↗ 500m

ℹ️ Mountain bike rental in Kiotári: *Dimitris Manias Rent a Motorbike (Kiotári Shopping Centre on the main street | tel. 22 44 04 70 20 | tel. 69 77 66 57 4)*
You should definitely reserve your bikes in advance!
Rental: approx. 12 euros/day
Take a picnic!

CYCLING FROM VILLAGE TO VILLAGE

From ❶ Kiotári ➤ p. 70 where you will start your trip in the morning, you should *follow the coast until you reach the northern edge of* ❷ Gennádi ➤ p. 72, a village that has retained its truly authentic character. *From here, the road towards Vatí, which is 7km away, forks off from the road circling the island* and leads into the middle of the island along a mostly flat stretch where, if you are lucky, you may spot deer. *You should definitely cycle into* ❸ Vatí *itself* because the village square is well worth a stop.

Afterwards, continue upwards through the hilly countryside, which was recently damaged by forest fires but is still full of fruit trees, *to the small church of* ❹ Agía Iríni and then pass by ❺ Taverna Vrisi *(open daily | tel. 22 44 06 11 78 | €)* with its simple, good country-style food. *Cycle on through* ❻ Arnithá with its abundance of flowers, the 19th-century Church of St George and an old drinking fountain.

❶ **Kiotári**

   4km 15mins

❷ **Gennádi**

   7km 25mins

❸ **Vatí**

   8km 30mins

❹ **Agía Iríni**

   2km 10mins

❺ **Taverna Vrisi**

   0.5km 4mins

❻ **Arnithá**

   12km 1½hrs

A WINDY TRACK WITH GREAT VIEWS

The most difficult stretch of the route lies ahead, but it also offers the best views. *The often dusty field track winds over the 500-m high Koukoúliari hills and after 12km you will come to* **⑦** Mesanagrós ➤ p. 77 with its ancient village church and the cosy tavern Kafeníon O Tsambíkos ➤ p. 77. After a long, incredibly relaxing break among the rather old villagers, head back at around 3pm along the last, mostly downhill stretch.

⑦ Mesanagrós
2km 10mins

PICNIC BY THE CHURCH

If you would prefer to have a picnic, the small pilgrimage church of **⑧** Ágios Thomás ➤ p. 78 *in the forest directly below the road to Lachaniá is the ideal place,* but please be aware that you won't find any drinking water here.

⑧ Ágios Thomás
6km 25mins

BLESSED ORGANIC VEGETABLES

On the way to the village of **⑨** Lachaniá ➤ p. 73 *you will have to manage just one more short ascent.* Right afterwards, you can stop in at Acropole chez Chrissis ➤ p. 73, the coffee house of the village priest, or treat yourself to some of the organic fruit and vegetables. The priest is more than willing to pose for a photo in his traditional robes.

⑨ Lachaniá
10km 35mins

No rush! The village square of Lachaniá is ideal for a relaxing stop

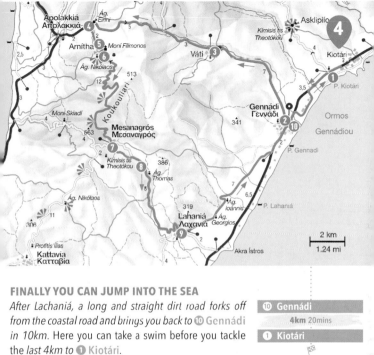

FINALLY YOU CAN JUMP INTO THE SEA

After Lachaniá, a long and straight dirt road forks off from the coastal road and brings you back to ⑩ Gennádi in 10km. Here you can take a swim before you tackle the *last 4km to ① Kiotári.*

⑩ Gennádi	
4km 20mins	
① Kiotári	

GOOD TO KNOW

HOLIDAY BASICS

ARRIVAL

GETTING THERE
There are direct charter flights from many British airports and most major cities in Western Europe. The flight time from London is around 4 hours. Passengers on scheduled flights (almost always) have to fly via Athens. Rhodes airport lies 14km to the south of the capital, Rhodes Town. There is a half-hourly bus service into town for (2.60 euros, while taxis cost approx. 30 euros and take around 25 minutes.

+ 2 hours ahead
Greece is two hours ahead of Greenwich Mean Time, seven hours ahead of US Eastern Time and seven hours behind Australian Eastern Time.

GETTING IN
A valid passport is required for entry into Greece (and for excursions into Turkey). Children need their own passport.

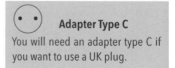
Adapter Type C
You will need an adapter type C if you want to use a UK plug.

CLIMATE & WHEN TO GO
With the exception of the rainy and stormy months between December and mid-March, any time is a good time to visit. The island's countryside is especially lush and in full bloom between March and May. Less colourful, perhaps, but still with pleasant water temperatures, October or November are also a good choice. July and August are least suitable for hikers and those interested in visiting cultural sites due to the heat.

Bear in mind that many archaeological sites, such as at Kámiros, offer no shade

GETTING AROUND

BUS & FERRY

Buses link almost all the villages around the island with Rhodes Town. The departure point for all buses is at the back of the Néa Agorá market hall. Rhodes Town is served by seven bus lines running between about 7am and 9pm. Up-to-date schedules can be obtained at tourist information offices and *ando.gr/eot*. In the summer months, a Sea Shuttle *(falirakisealines.com)* runs between Faliráki and Rhodes Town four times a day from Mondays to Saturdays.

CAR HIRE

Cars can be hired at the airport, in Rhodes Town and in all holiday resorts.

Drivers only need to hold a valid national driving licence. It is highly recommended to compare prices on the internet. Usually, Greek rental firms hand the hire vehicle over with an almost empty tank. You are expected to return it in the same state and will not get a refund for excess petrol in the tank.

The maximum speed is 50kmh in towns and 90kmh on national roads. Maximum blood alcohol content (BAC) is 0.05%. Right of way is not indicated as such – you will only recognise it by the Stop and Give Way signs on minor roads. At roundabouts, anything coming from the right has right of way, unless signposted otherwise.

In the event of a breakdown, you should contact the *Greek Automobile Association (ELPA |tel. 1 04 00)*. Car rental firms often have contracts with private recovery services.

TAXI

Taxis are to be found at the airport, outside the big hotels and at the taxi rank in Rhodes Town *(Mandráki Harbour | tel. 22 41 06 47 34 or tel. 22 41 06 47 12)*. You can also flag down taxis in the street. Current prices can be found at *ando.gr/eot*.

EMERGENCIES

CONSULATES & EMBASSIES
British Embassy (Athens)
1 Ploutarchou | 10675 Athens | tel. 21 07 27 26 00 | ukingreece.fco.gov.uk

Canadian Embassy (Athens)
48 Ethnikis Antistaseos Street | Chalandri | 15231 Athens | tel. 21 07 27 34 00 | www.international. gc.ca/country-pays/greece-grece

US Embassy (Athens)
91 Vasilisis Sophias | 10160 Athens | tel. 21 07 21 29 51 | gr.usembassy.gov

EMERGENCY SERVICES
Call 112 – for the police, fire brigade and ambulance.

HEALTH
Well-trained doctors guarantee basic medical care throughout Rhodes, however there is often a lack of technical equipment. If you are seriously ill, it is advisable to return home; make sure this will be covered by your travel insurance before you start your trip. Emergency treatment in hospitals is free of charge, and you can be treated for free by doctors if you present the European/Global Health Insurance Card. However, in practice doctors do so reluctantly and it is better to pay cash, get a receipt and then present your bills to the insurance company for a refund.

Most towns and villages have chemists *(farmakíon)* that are well-stocked, but they may not always have British medication.

ESSENTIALS

ACCOMMODATION
All coastal towns and also some of the villages inland offer accommodation of all sorts. For a real Rhodian experience, look for a place to stay in the Old Town of Rhodes or in the village of Líndos. There are no campsites or youth hostels on the island.

BEACHES
Many beaches are only cleaned in front of hotels and where sun loungers and parasols are for hire. Life guards are only found on highly frequented beaches and mainly during peak season. Seaweed that has been washed onto the beach at the beginning of the season is often only removed in May or June. Bathing shoes are recommended on many of the beaches (especially in summer when the sand tends to get extremely hot). bathing is prohibited, but is practised and tolerated on many isolated beaches. The only official nudist beach on Rhodes lies at the southern edge of Faliráki.

FESTIVALS & EVENTS
ALL YEAR ROUND

MARCH
Carnival Monday Colourful carnival celebrations in Archángelos.

Greek national holiday Laying of wreaths and parades across the island.

APRIL/MAY
Roads to Rhodes International marathon starting in Rhodes Town. *roadstorhodes.com*

Good Friday Processions in all towns and villages at 9pm (or at midnight in Archángelos).

Easter Saturday Easter mass from 11pm. Shortly before midnight, all lights in the churches across the island go out, except for the "eternal" sanctuary lamps. At midnight, the priests announce the Resurrection of Christ. The congregations light candles and outside there are firework displays.

Parish Fair of the Church of Ágios Thomás On Sunday after Easter in Mesanagrós.

Medieval Rose Festival Three-day event in Kritiniá on last weekend in May. *medievalfestival.gr*

JULY
Koskinoú Parish Fair A traditional gathering held on 16/17 July.

Profítis Ilías Parish Fair Traditional market and fair held in the evening of 19 July.

Parish Fair of the Ágios Syllas Monastery Music, dance and donkey racing near Soróni on 29 July.

AUGUST/SEPTEMBER
Festival of the Virgin Mary Celebrated 14–23 Aug in Kremastí with a fair, dance and music.

Wine Festival of Émbonas Late August/early September, with dance troupes from all over Rhodes.

Mass pilgrimage The path to Tsambíka Monastery is illuminated on evening of 7/8 September.

OCTOBER
Afántou Parish Fair 17/18 October.

DECEMBER
Christmas Market A romantic experience in Sálakos, from 23 December.

CUSTOMS
EU citizens can import and export for their personal use tax-free: 800 cigarettes, 1kg tobacco, 90 litres of wine, 10 litres of spirits (over 22 % vol.). Non-EU citizens can import and export for their personal use tax-free: 200 cigarettes, 250g tobacco, 4 litres of wine, 1 litre of spirits (over 22 % vol.), 16 litres of beer.

DRINKING WATER
You can drink the (chlorinated) tap water everywhere. Still mineral water *(metallikó neró)* is also available in restaurants and cafés and is usually the same price as in the supermarkets.

INFORMATION
Rhodes Tourist Information
Office *Néa Agorá, Averof 3 | tel. 22 41 03 59 45 | there is a notice board with ferry and bus time schedules in front of the building. Other offices are next to the Museum of Archaeology and inside the cruise ship terminal.*

Greek National Tourism
Organisation *5th floor East, Great Portland House, 4 Great Portland Street | W1W 8QJ | London | tel. +44 20 7495 9300 | www.visitgreece.gr*

MONEY
The national currency is the euro. It is possible to exchange money and cash traveller's cheques at banks and post offices. Opening times: *Mon–Thu 8am–2pm, Fri 8am–1:30pm.* You can also withdraw cash using your credit card at ATMs.

MUCH DOES IT COST?

Hire car	*From 25 euros per day for a small car*
Petrol	*1.65 euros per litre premium*
Coffee	*1.50–2.50 euros for a cup of mocha*
Snack	*2.50 euros for gyros and pitta bread*
Parasol	*6–10 euros for a parasol and two sun loungers*
Donkey ride	*6 euros per person in Líndos*

NATIONAL HOLIDAYS
The moveable feasts are scheduled according to the Julian calendar.

1 Jan	New Year's Day
6 Jan	Epiphany
25 March	Independence Day; Annunciation Day
March / April	Good Friday; Easter
1 May	Labour Day
June	Whitsun
15 Aug	Assumption Day
28 Oct	National Holiday
25 / 26 Dec	Christmas

POST
Post offices are generally open Mon–Fri 7.30am–3pm. The main Post Office in Rhodes Town *(Platía Dimarchíou | Mandráki)* stays open until 8pm. Longer opening hours apply in resorts.

PHONE & MOBILE PHONE
In some areas on the island, Turkish networks are stronger than Greek

ones; if you don't want to phone via Turkey, you must search for a different roaming partner manually.

Dialling codes: Greece 0030 followed by the telephone number. To call the UK, dial 0044; Ireland, 00353; the USA, 001; Australia, 0061; then dial the local code without "0" and then the individual number.

SHOPS

In the resorts shops are usually open daily 10am–11pm. In the towns and cities, shops with a predominantly local customer base are open Mon–Sat 10am–1.30pm on Tue, Thu, Fri 5.30–8pm.

TIPPING

Tips are only expected in very touristy places. Greeks tend to give generously; small tips under 50 cents are seen as an insult. Tips are left on the table when leaving.

INSIDER TIP
Just leave it

TOILETS

Toilets on Rhodes can come as a surprise. They can be very posh and equipped with the latest Italian sanitary installations, but in other places you would only want to use them in an emergency. Be aware that in *all* toilets you are not allowed to flush even toilet paper down the drain (use the bin provided); the paper clogs the narrow drains and septic tanks.

WIFI

Almost all hotels, bars, cafés and tavernas offer free WiFi.

WEATHER

■ High season
■ Low season

	JAN	FEB	MAR	APRIL	MAY	JUNE	JULY	AUG	SEPT	OCT	NOV	DEC
Daytime temperatures (°C)	15	16	17	21	25	30	32	33	29	25	21°	17°
Night-time temperatures (°C)	7	8	9	11	15	19	21	22	19	15	12°	9°
☀ Hours of sunshine per day	5	5	7	9	10	12	13	12	11	8	6	4
🌂 Rainfall days per month	14	10	8	3	3	0	0	0	1	6	7	13
≈ Sea temperature (°C)	17	16	16	17	19	21	23	25	24	22	20	18

☀ Hours of sunshine per day　　🌂 Rainfall days per month　　≈ Sea temperature (°C)

USEFUL WORDS & PHRASES

SMALLTALK

Yes/no/maybe	ne/'ochi/'issos	Ναι/ Όχι/Ισως
Please/Thank you	paraka'lo/efcharis'to	Παρακαλώ/ Ευχαριστώ
Good morning/good evening/goodnight!	kalli'mera/kalli'spera/ kalli'nichta!	Καλημέραμ/ Καλησπέρα!/ Καληνύχτα!
Hello/ goodbye (formal)/ goodbye (informal)!	'ya (su/sass)/ a'dio/ ya (su/sass)!	Γεία (σου/σας)!/ αντίο!/Γεία (σου/ σας)!
My name is …	me 'lene …	Με λένεÖ …
What's your name?	poss sass 'lene?	Πως σας λένε?
Excuse me/sorry	me sig'chorite/ sig'nomi	Με συγχωρείτε / Συγνώημ
Pardon?	o'riste?	Ορίστε?
I (don't) like this	Af'to (dhen) mu a'ressi	Αυτό (δεν) ουμ αρέσει

SYMBOLS

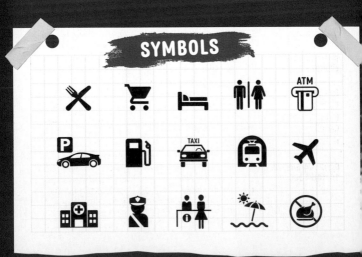

EATING & DRINKING

Could you please book a table for tonight for four?	Klis'te mass parakal'lo 'enna tra'pezi ya a'popse ya 'tessera 'atoma	Κλείστε αςμ παρακαλώ ένα τραπέζι γιά απόψε γιά τέσσερα άτοαμ
The menu, please	tonn ka'taloggo parakal'lo	Τον κατάλογο παρακαλώ
Could I please have … ?	tha 'ithella na 'echo …?	Θα ήθελα να έχω …?
more/less	pjo/li'gotäre	ρτιό/λιγότερο
with/without ice/sparkling	me/cho'ris 'pa-go/ anthrakik'ko	εμ/χωρίς πάγο/ ανθρακικό
(un)safe drinking water	(mi) 'possimo nä'ro	(μη) Πόσιμο νερό
vegetarian/allergy	chorto'fagos/allerg'ia	Χορτοφάγος/ Αλλεργία
May I have the bill, please?	'thel'lo na pli'rosso parakal'lo	Θέλω να πληρώσω παρακαλώ

MISCELLANEOUS

Where is …?	pu tha vro …?	Που θα βρω …?
What time is It?	Ti 'ora 'ine?	Τι ώρα είναι?
How much does... cost ?	Posso 'kani …?	Πόσο κάνει …?
Where can I find internet access?	pu bor'ro na vro 'prosvassi sto 'indernett?	Που πορώμ να βρω πρόσβαση στο ίντερνετ?
pharmacy/chemist	farma'kio/ ka'tastima	Φαρακείομ/ Κατάστηαμ καλλυντικών
fever/pain /diarrhoea/nausea	piret'tos/'ponnos/ dhi'arria/ana'gula	Πυρετός/Πόνος/ Διάρροια/Αναγούλα
Help!/Watch out! Be Careful	Wo'ithia!/Prosso'chi!/ Prosso'chi!	Βοήθεια!/Προσοχή!/ Προσοχή!
Forbidden/banned	apa'goräfsi/ apago'räwäte	Απαγόρευση/ απαγορέυεται
0/1/2/3/4/5/6/7/8/9/ 10/100/1000	mi'dhen / 'enna / 'dhio / 'tria / 'tessera / 'pende /'eksi / ef'ta / och'to / e'nea / dhekka / eka'to / 'chilia / 'dhekka chil'iades	ηδένμ/ένα/δύο/τρία/ τέσσερα/πέντε/έξι/ εφτά/οχτώ/ εννέα/ δέκα/εκατό/χίλια/ δέκα χιλιάδες

HOLIDAY VIBES

FOR RELAXATION & CHILLING

FOR BOOKWORMS & FILM BUFFS

🎥 THE GUNS OF NAVARONE

All-time classic from 1961, still rated as "one of the most exciting films ever made". It won an Oscar for its special effects. And the storyline? David Niven, Gregory Peck and Anthony Quinn fight the German occupiers; Irene Pappas plays the love interest.

📖 REFLECTIONS ON A MARINE VENUS

The quintessential Rhodes novel (1953): Lawrence Durrell paints a vivid picture of the island straight after World War II and before tourism arrived.

📖 RHODES 1306–1522: A STORY

Eureka! A both entertaining and informative book on the island's history in the age of the knights, narrated and illustrated by well-known caricaturist Vangélis Pavlídis. The book, which was published in 2001, is widely available on Rhodes.

📖 TRIANGLE AT RHODES

In this Agatha Christie short story, her famous Inspector Hercule Poirot investigates a crime on Rhodes. Also available as an audiobook, and a television episode from 1983.

PLAYLIST

♻ ◄ ❚❚ ► 🔊 ────

0:58

❚❚ **GIÓRGOS DALÁRAS –**
KÓKKINO TRIANDÁFILLOU
One of the best songs by the "Greek Bruce Springsteen".

▶ **MARÍA FANDOÚRI –** STIN ELLÁDA SÍMERA
The well-known singer performs this song by famous composer Míkis Theodorákis.

▶ **ÉLENA PAPARÍZOU –** MY NUMBER ONE
To date this has been Greece's only winning entry at the Eurovision Song Contest.

▶ **NÁNA MOÚSKOURI –** SUMMER HEART
The major star sings a romantic melody about Rhodes.

▶ **ROTTING CHRIST –** IN THE NAME OF GOD
Now it's getting loud and heavy: the Greek metal band is the antidote to any sensitive ballad.

*Your holiday soundtrack can be found on **Spotify** under **MARCO POLO** Greece*

Or scan this code with the Spotify app

ONLINE

RHODESGUIDE.COM
Information on accommodation, events and travel tips. Great photos and videos, too

MYLITTLENOMADS.COM
A section on "Rhodes with kids" provides tips, lists and personal advice specifically for family holidays.

FACEBOOK: LINDOS, RHODES
Líndos visitors swap news and views on various themes to do with Líndos. The notice board also features lots of tips and events.

CRUISETIMETABLES.COM
For anyone wanting to know more about the big cruise liners that come to Rhodes harbour every day and the implications on the numbers of visitors to the Old Town and Líndos.

MARINE TRAFFIC
The sea around the island gets very busy, and this app allows you to get information about the ships in your view and their routes.

TRAVEL PURSUIT

THE MARCO POLO HOLIDAY QUIZ

Do you know your facts about Rhodes? Here you can test your knowledge of the little secrets and idiosyncrasies of the island and its people. You will find the correct answers at the bottom of the page and in detail on pages 18 to 23 of this guide.

❶ What is the Rhodian name for a playboy or lothario? Here's a clue: it translates as "harpoon" in English.
a) Gigolo
b) Casanova
c) Kamáki

❷ Who or what is entéchno?
a) an engineer
b) a musical genre
a) a craftsman

❸ And what does the often-heard word entáxi mean?
a) Taxi!
b) Absolutely not
c) Okay

❹ Where did the knights of Rhodes relocate after their defeat by the Ottomans?
a) Malta
b) Cyprus
c) Mexico

❺ What is regarded as a symbol of luck on the island?
a) a knot
b) a fly agaric
c) an image of the pope

❻ What is the Greek word for a female saint?
a) Agía
b) Aghía
c) Ayía

What is this favourite café game?

❼ What name is given to the images of saints of the Orthodox Church which you can see everywhere?
a) Panini
b) Iconostases
c) Icons

❽ Which game do Rhodians love to play when meeting in a café?
a) Távli
b) Skat
c) Battleships

❾ For how long did the legendary Colossus of Rhodes stand at the entrance to the harbour?
a) 5 years
b) 50 years
c) 500 years

❿ And what was the statue predominantly made of?
a) Lego bricks
b) Bronze
c) Concrete

⓫ When did the Ottomans conquer Constantinople, the capital of the Byzantine Empire, which is now called Istanbul?
a) in 1054
b) in 1453
c) As late as 1912

⓬ How many nuclear power plants are on the sunny island of Rhodes?
a) None
b) One
c) Four

INDEX

INDEX & CREDITS

WE WANT TO HEAR FROM YOU!

Did you have a great holiday? Is there something on your mind? Whatever it is, let us know! Whether you want to praise the guide, alert us to errors or give us a personal tip – MARCO POLO would be pleased to hear from you.

We do everything we can to provide the very latest information for your trip. Nevertheless, despite all of our authors' thorough research, errors can creep in. MARCO POLO does not accept any liability for this. Please contact us by e-mail.

e-mail: sales@heartwoodpublishing.co.uk

Credits

Cover picture: Líndos, Hotel Interior (AWL: D. Pearson **Photos**: K. Bötig (127); W. Dieterich (6/7, 97); F.M. Frei (106); Getty Images: efilippou (2/3), J. Greuel (86/87), Maremagnum (43); R. Hackenberg (14/15, 98/99); huber-images: L. Da Ros (34/35, 78/79), D. Erbetta (95), S.&S. Grunig-Karp (back flap), Kaos03 (24/25), Schmid (26/27), R. Schmid (12/13, 52); Laif: J. Gläscher (10), B. Jaschinski (19); Laif/robertharding: N. Farrin (56/57); H. Leue (122/123); Look: I. Pompe (65), H. Wohner (64); Look/age fotostock (89); Lookphotos/Avalon.red (80/81); mauritius images (27, S. Beuthan (45, 84), P. Eastland (28), M. Habel (62), W. Layer (110); mauritius images/age (70/71); mauritius images/Alamy: R. Cracknell (51), T. Czajkowski (outside flap, inside flap, 1), I. Dagnall (22/23), D. Delimont (31), I. Eyewink (100/101), P. Forsberg (30/31, 48), N. Korzhov (46/47), L. Kovalic (90), L. Kovalik (9), C. Moustafellou (92), S. Outram (124/125), A. Starikov (58/59); mauritius images/Alamy/Geogphotos (66/67); mauritius images/Alamy/Hackenberg-Photo-Cologne (11, 72); mauritius images/Caia Image: T. Adeline (32/33); mauritius images/imagebroker: Ch. Handl (60, 112/113), M. Nitzschke (8); mauritius images/Radius Images (74/75); mauritius images/Westend61: T. Haupt (38/39); mauritius-images/Alamy/parasola.net (76); picture-alliance/akg-images (20); E. Wrba (44, 117)

3rd Edition - fully revised and updated 2022
Worldwide Distribution: Heartwood Publishing Ltd, Bath, United Kingdom
www.heartwoodpublishing.co.uk

© MAIRDUMONT GmbH & Co. KG, Ostfildern
Author: Klaus Bötig
Editor: Franziska Kahl
Picture editor: Ina-Marie Inderka
Cartography: © MAIRDUMONT, Ostfildern (pp. 36-37, 102, 105, 109, 113, outer flap, pull-out map) © MAIRDUMONT, Ostfildern, using data from OpenStreetMap, Licence CC-BY-SA 2.0 (pp. 40-41, 55, 60-61, 63, 82-83).
Cover design and pull-out map design: bilekjaeger Kreativagentur with Zukunftswerkstatt, Stuttgart
Page design: Langenstein Communication GmbH, Ludwigsburg

Heartwood Publishing credits:
Translated from the German by Susan Jones, Thomas Moser, Jane Riester, Jennifer Walcoff Neuheiser
Editors: Felicity Laughton, Kate Michell, Sophie Blacksell Jones
Prepress: Summerlane Books, Bath
Printed in India

MARCO POLO AUTHOR
KLAUS BÖTIG

A prolific travel-guide author, Klaus has known Rhodes for almost a lifetime, and he met his wife here. What he loves most about them both is their authenticity. Despite huge numbers of visitors to the island, Rhodians have kept their Greek identity, and this is because, although the island has always integrated change, it is deeply rooted in its 3,000-year history. *klaus-boetig.de.*

DOS & DON'TS

HOW TO AVOID SLIP-UPS & BLUNDERS

DO GO IT ALONE

Tour guides live partly off their commission, and the big tour operators factor them in from the beginning. However, remember you can, if you wish, book your own hire car or make your own way round the island via bus or taxi rather than going on organised excursions. Rhodes is in all respects a safe island, and there is no need to be wary of being independent.

DON'T SHOOT!

Many Rhodians enjoy being photographed, but hate it when tourists behave like hunters who shoot anything that moves! Before you take a picture, be sure to get permission with a smile first.

DON'T DRINK IF YOU DON'T WANT TO

Jewellers and leather salesmen like to treat potential customers to a glass of kir royale, whisky, oúzo or sparkling wine while making their sales pitch. Enjoy a glass if you wish, but remember it's not obligatory.

DO DRESS RESPECTFULLY

At the beach and in the tourist resorts Greeks have got used to the sight of plenty of bare skin. In the villages of the interior and in the Old Town, however, scanty clothing is inappropriate. In churches and monasteries, knees and shoulders must be covered, though it is not necessary for women to wear a headscarf.

DON'T BE SURPRISED AT THE PRICE OF FISH

Fresh fish is absurdly expensive in restaurants and tavernas in Greece. You should always ask the price per kilo and watch the fish being weighed in order to avoid unpleasant surprises when you get the bill.